DOCTOR WHO
WHO
THE WHAT WHERE AND HOW

Other Works by Valerie Estelle Frankel

Henry Potty and the Pet Rock: An Unauthorized Harry Potter Parody

Henry Potty and the Deathly Paper Shortage: An Unauthorized Harry Potter Parody

Buffy and the Heroine's Journey

From Girl to Goddess: The Heroine's Journey in Myth and Legend

Katniss the Cattail: An Unauthorized Guide to Names and Symbols in The Hunger Games

The Many Faces of Katniss Everdeen: Exploring the Heroine of The Hunger Games

Harry Potter, Still Recruiting: An Inner Look at Harry Potter Fandom

An Unexpected Parody: The Unauthorized Spoof of The Hobbit Movie

Teaching with Harry Potter

Myths and Motifs in The Mortal Instruments

Winning the Game of Thrones: The Host of Characters and their Agendas

Winter is Coming: Symbols, Portents, and Hidden Meanings in A Game of Thrones

Bloodsuckers on the Bayou: The Myths, Symbols, and Tales Behind HBO's True Blood

The Girl's Guide to the Heroine's Journey

Doctor Who and the Hero's Journey: The Doctor and Companions as Chosen Ones

DOCTOR WHO
THE WHAT WHERE AND HOW

A FANNISH GUIDE TO THE TARDIS-SIZED POP CULTURE JAM

Doctor Who – The What, Where, and How is an unauthorized guide and commentary on *Doctor Who* and its related universe. None of the individuals or companies associated with the books or television series or any merchandise based on this series have in any way sponsored, approved, endorsed, or authorized this book.

LitCrit Press

Contents

Why It's More than a Show 9

Huh? Deconstructing *Who* 13

    Retcon 18

    How Many Regenerations Does the Doctor Get? 21

    Books, Libraries, and Texts 24

    Troubles with the Idiot's Lantern 39

    Breaking the Fourth Wall 46

How We See Ourselves: Fan Episodes 53

    Creators as Fans 56

    The Doctor as Fan 58

    Companions as Fans 61

    The Doctor as Costumer 66

    Companions' Costumes 70

Who's Behind *Who* 75

    Creator References 75

    Cameos 84

    Actor References 86

Which Episodes Go Deeper: Self-Reference 95

    Old Who References in New Who 96

    New Who References in New Who 102

    Repeated Arc Words 104

The Expanded Universe Appears in Canon 108

Torchwood, Sarah Jane, and Who 112

What's Happening in the World: Pop Culture References . 115

Science Fiction 115

Fantasy 123

Classics 128

Religion 136

TV 139

Movies 143

Comics 149

Myth and Folklore 150

Music 156

Games 161

Other Series that Reference the Doctor 162

Where to Take Your Who Tour 167

London 167

Wales 168

Wales: Dining and Lodging 172

What Remains to be Said? 173

List of Doctors and Companions 175

Whoniverse Episode Guide 177

Bibliography 191

Glossary of Terms and Abbreviations 199

Index 205

Why It's More than a Show

"In a case of fiction eclipsing reality, the TARDIS displaces more cultural water than any genuine police box" (Newman 11). In fact, with fifty years of episodes, *Doctor Who* has had plenty of time to enter the cultural consciousness. Daleks appear on hundreds of shows and computer games, peeking from the windows of comic books or beeping on toy store shelves. But it's the references within the show that are truly intriguing, as it makes itself a show about books, reading, and authors; about the dangers of modern technology (even the television!); and a show about the actors, producers, and finally viewers. It's a program about ourselves, a cultural mirror defining who fandom is and what it can accomplish. *Doctor Who* is thus an "extended culture jam" designed to reclaim the public sphere "by turning the overblown ethos of mass consumption and corporate culture on its head," as Schuster and Powers explain in *The Greatest Show in the Galaxy: The Discerning Fan's Guide to Doctor Who* (9).

Russell T Davies, the man who revived *Doctor Who* in 2005, notes gleefully, "This programme gave me the chance to swing from New Labour to Dalek armies, taking in plastic surgery, Fox News, religious fanatics and farting obesity along the way, with a Christmas special to come (just wait till you see what we do with Santa)" ("Alien Resurrection," Kindle Locations 498-499). He included actors from his miniseries productions to play the Ninth and Tenth Doctors…and as they played a resurrected god and then the heartthrob that charmed all of Venice, these two characters found themselves reprising their roles in science fiction.

Fans of the geeky cult adventure they'd enjoyed in the

9

seventies and eighties were flabbergasted by its new popularity with the younger generation. Fifty years ago, it was a modest educational children's show in black and white, unrecordable as the technology didn't yet exist. Its short serials with hokey effects and low-budget costumes failed to suspend disbelief as warrior Daleks were thwarted by nonmagnetic floors. The show originally ran from 1963 to 1989, with a television movie that tried and failed to reboot the show in 1996. 2005 marked a new reboot, which continued right where the movie had left off as the Ninth Doctor strode into London. The original show lasted 26 "seasons," while the term "series" is now used for a year of a show in Britain. Thus the show went from Season 26 to Series 1, and so on. In 2006-2007, spin-offs *Torchwood* and *The Sarah Jane Adventures* began, both helmed by Davies during the Tennant era.

> Over the past few years, however, the profile of the Doctor has gradually, but perceptibly, grown on these shores – thanks in large part to BBC America, which secured the U.S. rights in 2009 and began broadcasting episodes on the same day they aired in the U.K. The cast has also repeatedly hopped the pond to shoot scenes – including for last season's premiere, partly shot in Utah – and publicize the show. Who's exec producer Steven Moffat and his stars attended this year's Comic-Con, where the enormous popularity of Gillan's leggy, red-haired Amy Pond was confirmed by the number of people who wore ginger wigs to the Who panel. The sixth-season premiere of *Doctor Who,* which was broadcast in June of last year, garnered an audience of 1.3 million – the highest ratings BBC America has seen. *Doctor Who* also beat out *Dexter* and *Modern Family* to become 2011's most downloaded series on iTunes. "It's not an obscure show anymore," says [current showrunner Steven] Moffat. "It's not even 'a British import' – it's just 'Doctor Who.'" (Collis, "The Doctor is In")

Today, there are fan tours of Rose Tyler's favorite café and Sarah Jane's home on Bannerman Road. There's Time Lord Rock – fan music to accompany the fan films, costumes, art, Etsy products, and extensive merchandising surrounding the show. There are hundreds of novelizations and audio adventures, thousands of fanfiction stories. Conventions like Gallifrey One and Chicago TARDIS bulge with costumed teens and adults, to say nothing of Comic-Con itself.

Eleventh Doctor Matt Smith debuted at Comic-Con in 2011, surrounded by fans dressed as everything from TARDISes to Weeping Angels. "It's really exciting for us to see," says Smith of the series' growing American success. "It's kind of wonderful to be part of a legacy in *Doctor Who* and to be part of something that has such history. It's remarkable" (Child). Most creators are in fact fans, who approach the show with devotion. David Tennant, the Tenth Doctor, grew up watching his heroes before he got to act alongside several of them, like the Fifth Doctor and Sarah Jane Smith. Alex Kingston used to watch the Second Doctor, and never expected to be kissing a later version (Hickman 96).

As the show prepares for its twelfth Doctor, and a new era once more, it continues to grow and shift, while still remaining lively, with the new grandiose story arcs that characterize the Moffat era. As John Tulloch and Manuel Alvarado acknowledge in *Doctor Who: The Unfolding Text*: "*Doctor Who* represents a site of endless transformations and complex weavings as well as a programme of increasing institutional stability and public popularity" (5-6).

This book takes a look at the show as self-referential fiction, as a show about television and fiction itself as it borrows, steals, and lovingly acknowledges the other works surrounding its creation.

Huh? Deconstructing *Who*

On one level, this is the story of a man and a human companion adventuring through time and space in a big blue box. Sure. But to some fans, something's missing.

By the time of *New Who,* the Doctor addresses why he has adventures on Saturdays, why the show is named *Doctor Who* – "The ultimate question…hidden in plain sight" and whether, in a world of committing genocide against the alien races to protect humans (in "The Vampires of Venice," "The Beast Below" and "The Satan Pit," among others), he's doing as much good as he thinks. The events of the show reflect its screening, cancelation, and even titles, playing with the audience while acknowledging their presence. Other running jokes and mentions continue to attack the show's very premise or call attention to it, examining the show as if tugging at loose threads:

- In several episodes, the Doctor mentions the faulty chameleon circuit…River and the Doctor-Donna even offer to fix it for him. Obviously, that would destroy the most iconic part of the show, so the Doctor firmly refuses.
- "Time isn't a straight-line. It's all…bumpy-wumpy. There's loads of boring stuff, like Sundays and Tuesdays and Thursday afternoons. But now and then there are Saturdays. Big temporal tipping points when anything's possible. The TARDIS can't resist them. Like a moth to a flame" ("The Impossible Astronaut"). Doctor Who premiers on Saturdays, apparently the day when momentous things happen in the universe.

- *Doctor Who* is filmed in Cardiff, with a wink to the audience during the Slitheen's speech of "Boom Town": "It's *Cardiff*. London doesn't care! The entire west coast could fall into the sea and they wouldn't notice."
- "The Last of the Time Lords" ends with Martha's departure, then the Titanic crashing through the TARDIS. Later, the minisode "Time Crash" was added between these two scenes, as Colin Baker briefly returns in a time paradox threatening to destroy reality. This only makes sense if time is being rewritten, in a self-referential science fiction moment.
- "When Christopher Eccleston's 9th Doctor memorably stumbles into his TARDIS in the 2005 episode "Father's Day" (written by Paul Cornell), only to find it has transmuted into an actual police telephone box, he is shocked along with viewers because it subverts our prior knowledge of the television show – The TARDIS itself carries mythic status within the wider culture," notes C. B. Harvey in "Canon, Myth, and Memory in *Doctor Who*" (29). This is a symbol of the show and *cannot* be destroyed…though apparently it has been.
- As the Doctor dies in "The End of Time," Ood Sigma tells him that "this song is ending, but the story never ends," which works as a reference to the show's longevity.
- In the Pandorica arc, the universe was scheduled to blow up on June 26th 2010, the day the last episode of that series aired.
- Russell T. Davies assaults the idea of the Doctor himself in "Midnight," in which all of the Doctor's normal strategies backfire, and he fails to save the day, and then is almost killed himself. Characters like the last Dalek and his daughter Jenny point out that as a soldier, he's not so different from them. In "Journey's End" and "A Good Man Goes to War," his enemies reveal that he is not the pacifist and do-gooder he had imagined himself. It's finally revealed that the doctor's enemies are so

14

frightened of him that they commit terrible acts (like kidnapping baby Melody and creating the Pandorica) just to be rid of him.

- The *Brilliant Book 2012* reveals that Mels (like Susan) adopted a surname while she was living on Earth. Mels' surname - "Zucker" - means "sugar" in German, it ties in very nicely with her catchphrase of "Sweetie" (102).

- In the original era, the title had no bearing on the plot...in early episodes, the closing credits name the Doctor as "Doctor Who" in truth. Moffat has reimagined this into "The ultimate question, hidden in plain sight" (literally, as it's on the title screen), and a question worth destroying reality over. Characters ask the signature question all the time (especially in "The Snowmen"), and the Doctor reflects on his name meaning as he considers betraying his name in "The Beast Below" or discovers it's the word for warrior on one planet after he passed through.

- By the Time War, the Eighth Doctor realizes that his identity as a Time Lord has made him a hated figure – calling himself the Doctor and "one of the nice ones" isn't enough to set him apart. Thus, in "The Night of the Doctor," he commits to war and redefines himself.

The reboot also addresses many unexplored aspects of the Doctor's dynamic – Rose's and Amy's families worry about what they've gotten into, as do Martha and Donna's in different ways. For the first time, consequences appear as Rose and the Doctor return to chaos a year after leaving: the cops demand to know if the Doctor whisked her away for a sexual relationship, missing persons investigations have begun, and Jackie is frantic. Thus a bit of reality enters the magical adventures.

The Doctor is not always the safe alien. He is threatening when seen from the other human perspectives of Mickey and Jackie, Rose's friend and mother. He took Rose away for over a year, leading Mickey to be suspected of her disappearance and Jackie to be left alone. In "Aliens of London," Mickey says, "You look deep enough on the

> Internet, or in the history books, and there's his name…with a list of the dead." This points to the importance of considering standpoint for the experience of insecurity – for some (humanity, as represented by Harriet Jones), the Doctor (an alien) is a savior or, for Rose, a source of adventure and new experiences. For others, such as Jackie and Mickey, he is a threat to their families and way of life.…This duality in the Doctor's identity draws attention to the importance of standpoint; meanings of "security" and "threats" depend on whose perspective we foreground. (Dixit 294)

The series also comments on its nature as television – television that in *Who's* case can vanish if not archived properly. As the Doctor travels to a planet-sized storage archive in the Library or Clara roams the Doctor's life from beginning to end, the concept of saving all the parts of the story becomes paramount. This reflects fans' dismay over the infamous "lost episodes": In the First and Second Doctor eras, tapes were recycled to save money, then deliberately deleted as the producers assumed fans would prefer the new color film beginning with the Third Doctor's era. (They also lacked various rights to rebroadcast without renegotiating with actors.) It was a different world, without home video. "Until 1981, viewers were absolutely *sure* that any given episode of *Doctor Who* was something they'd only be able to witness once" (Wood and Miles 143).

Only in 1978, after establishing the BBC Film and Videotape Library, did the BBC begin searching for and preserving the lost episodes. In 1983, a total of 134 episodes were "missing, believed lost," and over the next 21 years, only 26 were retrieved (Chapman 203-204). (Episodes in this case refer to individual sections of four-part or sometimes six-part serials. For many episodes, one or more parts have been saved and other parts may have been reconstructed in cartoons or other mediums.) Today, fans are scouring other countries, seeking the copies the BBC sent to far-off television stations. By the time of the fiftieth anniversary, 97 episodes still remained lost though fans were celebrating the sudden discovery of "The

Enemy of the World" and "The Web of Fear" – the latter featuring the first appearance of beloved Brigadier Lethbridge-Stewart. Transcripts, novelizations, and fan-made audio recordings remain, but this is a blow for those longing to watch the originals.

As the self-referential world of analysis grows ever-deeper, the lost episodes themselves have gained prominence in fan culture:

> Legends persist of wealthy misanthropes holding episodes hostage or greedily enjoying private screenings as true fans went without. It is this mythic caricature, rather than "Doctor Who's" very real grey-suited state-employed despoilers, that passes for the story's villain. The copious online literature covering the lost episodes exhibits meticulous knowledge of such minutiae as which episode marks the last of the 405-line screen transmissions and which heralds the beginning of 625-line video. But talk of bullying unions or state malfeasance is missing from the conversation about missing "Doctor Who" stories. Leave it to science-fiction fans to exhibit supersized imaginations, as capable of envisioning a secret society of aristocrats squirreling away lost pop-culture artifacts as they are of anticipating something that has been lost for decades showing up the day after tomorrow. (Flynn)

In another terribly self-referential moment, the American-produced Eighth Doctor from the movie was not clearly defined as legitimate among the television Doctors' progressions (though the Seventh Doctor was seen becoming him). Many did not consider him canon at all until he showed up in flashbacks on "The Next Doctor" and "The Eleventh Hour" as well as the Doctor's sketches in "Human Nature." However, these episodes themselves are subject to scrutiny and "rewriting of time," suggesting more than initially appears. "Interestingly, the 8th Doctor is portrayed via representative modes...in other words, as memories, which we might read and accept as liable to being misremembered, as opposed to flashbacks in which diegetic truth is portrayed," C.B. Harvey notes in his essay, "Canon, Myth, and Memory in *Doctor Who*." "In fact, both 'Human

17

Nature' and 'The Next Doctor' concern themselves with the problems of memory as a central theme, and problems of remembering and misremembering can be perceived as a recurring concern for the Cardiff-produced series" (Harvey 30).

In other words, since he's shown up as fuzzy uncertain memories, or in databases which soon are wiped (in the events of "Asylum of the Daleks") the canon remains uncertain, and some would call McGann a "fuzzy" incarnation of the Doctor. This is an idea further reinforced by the BBC's official *Doctor Who* website, intoned by an authoritative but otherwise unidentified female voice-over: "The 8th Doctor's first adventure was to save Earth at the end of the twentieth century. There are many stories told about what happened next, but due to the Time Wars we don't know how many are true." (*The Beginner's Guide to Doctor Who*). Indeed, the Time Wars serve an important role for many fan commentators in helping explain away inconsistencies through the series, and offer a potential loophole for more problematic works that might otherwise prove too contradictory to include. If all of time was rewritten, well, vanished episodes and inconsistencies may no longer exist. If the Daleks can be unwritten from time, why shouldn't they have conflicting origin stories as well?

The Ninth Doctor may seem like a fresh start for fans, but the unseen Time War is a never-ending font of baggage. "Bored with his home planet and something of a rebel among the Time Lords, the Doctor always seemed content with himself. Since the final Time War, however…the Doctor is now fully self-directed and painfully alone" (Akers 146). Though he gains a companion and travels with her as usual, the happy-go-lucky attitude of the earlier Doctors appears marred by grief and guilt, as well as a terrible rage at the Daleks. As such, the Ninth Doctor starts in the middle of a story in more ways than one.

Retcon

With changing concepts and writers through the fifty year series, there's been a great deal of retcon. This is a fannish term short for Retroactive Continuity Change, contradicting a fact from an earlier episode. Some of the more ambitious fans have tried to accept all the versions as true and make them all make sense in context, creating guides like the online *Cloister Library* and *Discontinuity Guide* or the celebrated book *Doctor Who: A History of the Universe* by *Who* novelist Lance Parkin.

- Early closing credits, and episodes such as "Doctor Who and the Silurians" suggested "Doctor Who" is actually the main character's name.
- The Daleks originally hide in their city for a few centuries waiting for their world to become habitable. They need radiation to survive and can only operate their "travel machines" on powered metal surfaces. They are not terribly intelligent or powerful – the Doctor soundly defeats them. Their flight and devastating military might come later, as does their time travel. Their creation by Davros only appeared in the Fourth Doctor's era.
- The Time War allegedly wiped Time Lords and Daleks from all of history; however, most characters remember Time Lords as a legend at least. While the Daleks apparently vanished from existence, they reappear in many episodes through various excuses. Everyone in the universe appears to remember them as well.
- No one in the new show seems to recall aliens flattening London all the time – this is addressed multiple times as the Doctor bemoans humanity's capacity for self-delusion.
- The Cybermen only gain their trademark appearance in their fifth episode, "The Invasion" (Second Doctor) and only gain a weakness to gold in "Revenge of the Cybermen." However, *New Who's* Cybermen are excused from the rules, as they come from an alternate dimension.
- Susan claims she invented the term TARDIS in the show's first episode, but other Time Lords use it too.

- The Doctor visits three incompatible versions of "the real Atlantis" on the old series.
- The Doctor meets several historical characters, like Shakespeare, who should remember him from a previous adventure but don't.
- Mels's entire existence and backstory with Amy and Rory appears in a lengthy retcon montage, inserting her in their history and clumsily explaining why she's never appeared on the show before.
- The American-produced Eighth Doctor from the movie describes himself as "half human," a phrase that fans can't explain (though they've tried) unless he's lying, mistaken, or confused, or this regeneration brought him back as the wrong species.

Several more deliberate moments of Retcon or bandage-like explanations have appeared on the show as it actually uses broken rules as a storytelling tool:

- The concept that "Time can be rewritten" suggests multiple contradictory origin stories and histories *could* be true, as time is always changing.
- Rose can never leave her alternate universe and never be with the Doctor. However, she slips through in the fourth series (in multiple trips!) and is given a Doctor-copy. It's explained that reality is breaking down.
- Steven Moffat has reportedly said that, as a result of the cracks in the universe, the various alien invasions were erased from history and wiped from the public's mind. This concept appears in "The Eleventh Hour" and as critic Kevin Mahoney puts it in *Steven Moffat's Doctor Who 2010*, "Moffat seems to be recalibrating the world of the show away from the situation that developed over the last five years, where pretty much everyone in the world was aware of both the existence of aliens and the organizations that deal with them" (Cooper and Mahoney 14). The new world, repaired through Amy's imagination, may be subtly different.

- In "Asylum of the Daleks," the Doctor was erased from every database ever, so nobody remembers him. Presumably he will grow from a man with a terrifying reputation to an eccentric shadow, surprising people wherever he goes.
- The Tenth Doctor suddenly reveals in "The Stolen Earth" that the TARDIS is meant to be piloted by six people. Through the early seasons, the Doctor had little-to-no control over his ship, which flew him about randomly. The revelation of "The Doctor's Wife" that the TARDIS is alive and taking him "where he needs to go" also helps explain its behavior.
- "Time Crash" and other episodes reference "changing the desktop theme" of the TARDIS console room, explaining the radically different looks. It's implied the ability has always been around, though no one in the sixties would have used such a phrase.
- Idris insists that the TARDIS doors were meant to swing out in "The Doctor's Wife." This explains occasions like on "The Eleventh Hour" and "The Ice Warriors," in which the doors in fact swung out.
- The *Torchwood* show plays with the fannish concept, making the drug "retcon" that they give people to make them forget Torchwood's existence. In "Something Borrowed," Jack uses a very particular form of the drug, implying people will hazily remember Gwen's wedding as normal, rather than disrupted by an alien pregnancy – an unlikely drug indeed.

How Many Regenerations Does the Doctor Get?

Tennant noted when he took the role, 'Time Lords can only have 13 bodies, but I'm sure when they get to that they can find some storyline where he falls in a vat of replenishing cream or something" (Merritt, Kindle Locations 652-654). Officially speaking, it is stated in "The Deadly Assassin" of 1976 that Time Lords can only regenerate 12 times, for a total of 13 "lives." In December 2013, the Twelfth Doctor will appear, suggesting the show's span is limited. But anyone who watches science fiction knows there's always a way.

Several episodes have explicitly numbered the Doctors we know as one through eleven, though again, the canon has a bit of flexibility. The First Doctor is only *assumed* to be the first, and the transitions from the Second to Third and the Eighth to Ninth Doctors weren't shown. "The Brain of Morbius" reveals what *might* be earlier faces of the Doctor (in a self-referential moment, they're actually photos of directors Christopher Barry and Douglas Camfield and script editor Robert Holmes, among others). Nonetheless, the list of the Doctors is well-established (after fifty years, no one wants to renumber them all!) and television has supported the official count. In "The Name of the Doctor," for instance, Clara says, "I saw all of you. Eleven faces, all of them you! You're the eleventh Doctor!"

Nonetheless, even on the show, the twelve regenerations don't seem hard and fast. Once again, various levels of inconsistency and rewriting emerge. The "regeneration cycle" of a Time Lord can be transferred to other Time Lords, reduced, or increased. In "Trial of a Time Lord," the Valeyard is bribed with his former self's remaining lives. In the movie, the Master tries to steal the Doctor's lives. When the Master returns in "Utopia," he reveals he's been given a new regeneration cycle (presumably 13 lives) to fight in the Time War. In the old series, he's bribed with lives and finally steals a new body, confusing the count beyond measure. In a different type of example, River gives all of hers up to save the Doctor, and gets angry when he uses some of his to heal her broken wrist (both are concepts not fully explained). Thus the Doctor could steal lives or receive them as a gift (a problem with no more Time Lords around, admittedly). Visiting *The Sarah Jane Adventures,* he tells Clyde he can regenerate 507 times, but it's likely he's joking. Some fans have noted one can add the digits and get twelve – he may be hiding his vulnerability in code.

Regeneration was invented when the First Doctor's actor wanted to leave the show. However, many aspects of the process grew organically or became contradictory. In "Power of the Daleks," the Second Doctor describes regenerating as a function of his TARDIS, but other episodes show him or the Master regenerating far away. The Time Lords force a regeneration on the Second Doctor, who complains, "You can't just change what I look like without consulting me!" By the Tenth Doctor's time, this would be described as an execution. He explains, "I can still die. If I'm killed before regeneration, then I'm dead. Even then, even if I change, it feels like dying. Everything I am dies. Some new man goes sauntering away, and I'm dead" ("The End of Time: Part One").

Even beyond this, there has been rule-breaking for the purpose of the story. In "The Stolen Earth"/"Journey's End," the Doctor oddly halts the process and (presumably) doesn't use up a life, though he creates a duplicate of himself. In "Destiny of the Daleks" the Time Lady Romana undergoes a voluntary regeneration and tries out several forms as if dress shopping before settling on the appearance of a woman she recently met. This incident contradicts most known rules, though Romana may have a particular talent or better technology for regenerating because of her youth or for another reason.

Neil Gaiman, author of many bestselling novels as well as episodes "The Doctor's Wife" and "Nightmare in Silver" explains:

> It's interesting, that rule. It was obviously bendable to begin with (the Time Lords gave the Master a whole new round of regenerations). So I've always thought that it was more a law like a speed limit is a law than like Gravity is a law. And if there are no longer any police to make you observe the speed limit, you can drive as fast as you like. Although it's a lot more dangerous. And that's my opinion. As to what Mr Moffat thinks, he may either have a plan, or he may figure it's not his problem, but is one for eight or ten years down the line. (Q & A: Neil Gaiman)

Books, Libraries, and Texts

> SHAKESPEARE: And you, Sir Doctor. How can a man so young have eyes so old?
> DOCTOR: I do a lot of reading. ("The Shakespeare Code")

The show reboots by describing the Doctor as "a legend woven throughout history," as history and the companions see him. "The *Doctor Who* series has always been surrounded by an array of texts, some official, some not, since its inception in 1963" (Berger 66). Episodes were novelized directly, until 1991 when independent Who adventures appeared as well. Over 50,000 works of fanfiction crowd the web, half of which focus on the Tenth Doctor. But that's nothing compared to the number of books to be found within the Doctor's universe, from the novelizations and comics of his adventures to the many classics he's seen reading and quoting. All Eleven Doctors star in over two hundred original novels, including the Missing Adventures and New Adventures series. Big Finish Productions has created hundreds of audio adventures, often recorded by the actual Doctors' and companions' actors. There have been plays and fan films, short stories and long graphic novels. The Eighth Doctor, though only present onscreen for the American-made TV movie, has several long series of adventures, with new companions in audio and text.

"*Who* has always been intertextual: the new series made overt references to not only its own back-story and history but also to other texts such as Douglas Adams' *Hitchhiker's Guide to the Galaxy* series and even the Disney film *The Lion King* (Berger 69). It's a show about books and the power of words, over and over, as the characters explore libraries in the depth of space or deep within the TARDIS, discovering the awesome mysteries their favorite character buries just as deep within himself. As the characters journey through worlds of books and meet writers and fictional characters, they remind the audience that this too is a work of fiction – one that reaches wisdom by laughing at itself.

Matt Smith, discussing his role as the Eleventh Doctor,

reveals, "The script is where it starts, it's always about the words, and luckily we're in the hands of Steven Moffat, who has this show ingrained in his soul and searing through his blood...I really responded to Steven's writing – it gives you so much" (Cook).

Critic David Layton notes that many *Who* episodes resemble fairytales, both with good triumphing over evil and sometimes with their specific trappings.

> In "Terror of the Autons," (1971), plastic chairs, dolls, flowers, and even telephone wires come to life. "The Web Planet" (1965) features intelligent, human-sized insects. "The Trial of a Timelord: Attack of the Vervoids" (1986) has talking carnivorous plants. Two stories in particular, "The Celestial Toymaker (1966) and "The Mind Robber" (1968), expressly take place in malleable fairylands where rules of causality are suspended. (Humanism, 130)

Added to this list are the plastic Santas of "The Christmas Invasion" and "The Runaway Bride," children's drawings of "Fear Her" or dolls in "Night Terrors," and many children's adventures such as "The Rings of Akhaten" or "The Beast Below."

In "Journey to the Centre of the Tardis," Clara discovers the TARDIS library. Gazing at its towering stories of books, Gothic arches, and gleaming light, she mutters, "Now that's just showing off." Of course, fans' mouths watered as they admired the *Encyclopedia Gallifrey* stored in speaking bottles and the *History of the Time War,* which Clara manages to leaf through.

In the episode, the TARDIS sends the Doctor a written message, actually burning the words "Big Friendly Button" into Clara's palm. Words have a great deal of power in this episode: The doctor's threat that he'll overload the engines turns real. Two brothers lie and tell the third he's an android and the lie defines his life. And Clara's words instantly take form.

> DOCTOR: So, so the fuel's spilled out, so the rods will be exposed. Means they'll cool
> CLARA: And start to warp.

> DOCTOR: And start to warp. Maybe even –
> CLARA: No, you don't say it. Don't you dare say it!
> DOCTOR: Maybe even break apart.
> (A rod flies through the walls just in front of them.)

Memories and *Doctor Who* history are central to the episode – we hear the Cloister bell (seen in old series episodes) and hear the voices of old companions, even back to 1963's Susan and Ian. At the episode's climax, the Doctor tells Clara the truth about how he knows her and the copies of her he's encountered. The Doctor's line, "Secrets protect us, secrets make us safe" ties in with his personality. Clara in turn appears to discover his real name and deeds in *The History of the Time War*, a book in the TARDIS library. However, her memory, like the day, is rewritten.

> CLARA: What are you going to do?
> DOCTOR: Rewrite today, I hope.
> (He uses the sonic screwdriver to etch the letters onto the grenade.)
> DOCTOR: I've thrown this through the rift before. I need to make sure this time. Going to take it in there myself. There might be a certain amount of yelling.
> CLARA: It's going to hurt?
> DOCTOR: Things that end your life often do that.
> CLARA: Wait! All those things you said. How we've met before, how I died.
> DOCTOR: Clara, don't worry. You'll forget. Time mends us. It can mend anything.
> CLARA: I don't want to forget. Not all of it. The library. I saw it. You were mentioned in a book.
> DOCTOR: I'm mentioned in a lot of books.
> CLARA: You call yourself Doctor. Why do you do that? You have a name. I've seen it. In one corner of that tiny –
> DOCTOR: If I rewrite today, you won't remember. You won't go looking for my name.
> CLARA: You'll still have secrets.
> DOCTOR: It's better that way. ("Journey to the Centre of the Tardis")

They end the episode reset yet trusting each other and their

TARDIS a bit more. This episode sets up the importance of the Doctor's name and the secret behind it: Significantly, when the Doctor "meets himself," he calls himself Doctor – the person he wants to be.

In "Silence in the Library"/"Forest of the Dead," the Tenth Doctor visits the Library, which contains every book ever published, a concept popular in science fiction and fantasy. He explains:

> It's a world. Literally, a world. The whole core of the planet is the index computer. Biggest hard drive ever. And up here, every book ever written. Whole continents of Jeffrey Archer, Bridget Jones, Monty Python's Big Red Book. Brand new editions, specially printed. ("Silence in the Library")

Library planets brimming with all the known books in the universe also appear in the novel *Spiral Scratch* (Sixth Doctor) and the comics *War of the Words* (Fourth Doctor), *Hunger from the Ends of Time* (Seventh Doctor) and *The Time Machination* (Tenth Doctor). This concept demonstrates authors' love of books, as well as the Doctor's. As he explains, "Books. People never really stop loving books. Fifty first century. By now you've got holovids, direct to brain downloads, fiction mist, but you need the smell. The smell of books, Donna. Deep breath" ("Silence in the Library"). Of course, the Doctor is mentioned in these books and a walking work of fiction himself. In the episode, his new companion of a sort River Song (Alex Kingston) defines the Doctor as "The only story you'll ever tell, if you survive him" ("Silence in the Library"). In fact, he uses the library as a weapon, telling the shadow creatures:

> Tenth Doctor: I'm the Doctor, and you're in the biggest library in the universe. Look me up.
> (There is a pause, and then the shadows withdraw.)
> Shadows: You have one day. ("Forest of the Dead")

Unfortunately, the library's desire for real paper books created the episode's monsters. The Doctor notes, "The forests of the Vashta Nerada, pulped and printed and bound. A million, million books, hatching shadows" ("Forest of the Dead"). Only the computer's desperation to save everything – even people – proves everyone's salvation. By the time the two-part episode has ended, his friends Donna and River have been saved in the library as data, just like a book or television episode. This is an intriguing moment of narrative for viewers despondent over the missing episodes of *Doctor Who* – all information is worthy of being preserved.

Books, reading, and writing characterize the Doctor and River's romance, from their meeting in the Library to her death in the same episode and her final appearance in "The Name of the Doctor." In both, a companion is turned into data, though the Doctor manages to save her. The Doctor unravels the essential mystery of an important woman in his life – River or Clara. On the planet of Trenzalore, a name almost as secret as the Doctor's own, the Doctor battles information incarnate, the Great Intelligence. Clara, transformed into information as the Great Intelligence is, revisits scenes from the Doctor's life, spiraling through his stories beginning with a scene before his first episode, in which he steals the TARDIS. In both, the Doctor's name is used as a password and symbol of trust, offered by River. Jessica Burke explains in "Doctor Who and the Valkyrie Tradition," that River is more all-powerful seer than companion, because she understands the name's significance.

> Beforehand, expressing regret, she reflects even more intimate knowledge that his name isn't only a secret, but a source of pain for him. Apologizing, her hand on his heart, she momentarily fetters him in fear and disbelief. Pervaded with grief, face bathed in silver and red light, she names him, and he is speechless. (158)

In other adventures, River and the Doctor compare journals or she sends him messages, from a High Gallifreyan inscription in a museum to "The very first words in recorded history," inscribed on the ancient diamond cliffs of Planet One ("Hello Sweetie"). *The Brilliant Book 2012* features a school essay by

"Mels Zucker" in which she dreams of marrying the Doctor and traveling through time and space with him (102).

> It would appear that she's predestined to marry the Doctor, as well as kill him, along with adopting the name of River Song. The Doctor then actively encourages this mythmaking, as he gives her the "TARDIS blue" book of spoilers at the end of this episode. The Doctor knows that River will use it to record her adventures with him. As we know from 2008's Forest of the Dead, the Doctor left this diary in the biography section of the 51st century library that featured in that story – although this library had few visitors, who knows who could have read it after he left? (Mahoney 2011, 134)

The twin journals become a major plot point as well as a running joke – River uses them to foreshadow the Pandorica and the crash of the Byzantium. Likewise, the Doctor gives River hers when she first becomes River Song, and he leaves it behind when she dies – it's constructed as part of her identity. Burke adds, "We haven't been privy to any sharing of 'diaries' before. So, not only does River become his wife, she becomes his confidante, his Companion, and, in some ways, his biographer" (159). He adds:

> River's knowledge, her prophecy is exclusive to the Doctor – our hero – in the form of her little, blue, book, uncannily similar in appearance to the TARDIS. She also is able to contact him, to "call" him via his Psychic Paper. This time, the message arrived too early in his timeline, but we don't rightly discover why she called him. In addition to her book of prophecy, her "spoilers," she grants us a picture of the future Doctor. (Burke 159)

"People can find the Doctor through the stories that are told about him…We also know that River will pore through historical sources in her bid to find the Doctor, and she may even publish papers about him, so spreading his myth further," Kevin Mahoney adds (Cooper and Mahoney 2011, 134). In fact, the Doctor's and River's biographies, which they read, in "Let's

Kill Hitler," reveal their entwined fates of marriage and murder to come. She offers her love along with the love of the galaxy in their wedding episode, all through the message she sends. As she explains:

> I've been sending out a message. A distress call. Outside the bubble of our time, the universe is still turning, and I've sent a message everywhere. To the future and the past, the beginning and the end of everything. The Doctor is dying. Please, please help....The sky is full of a million, million voices saying yes, of course we'll help. ("The Wedding of River Song")

Spoilers are constantly threatened in the Doctor and River's relationship in a delightful moment of metanarrative – it's River's tagline, given to her by the Doctor after she gave it to him in a delightful loop. In the early days of internet fandom, those posting on fansites and in newsgroups would post the warning "SPOILER ALERT" before revealing crucial information. One of the first print uses of "spoilers" was in the April 1971 issue of *National Lampoon,* in which the article "Spoilers," by Doug Kenney, listed spoilers for famous films (Kenney).

There have been many real-life incidents with spoilers: show creators Davies and Moffat have bemoaned the fact that new companions and Doctors are heavily publicized, leaving no room for surprises. Moffat comments, "It was Russell's plan not to tell anyone that Chris [Eccleston] was going to change in the last episode, but it leaked after one week" (Radish, "Matt Smith"). Following this, Davies began releasing incomplete episodes for review, which allowed some events, such as Rose's cameo in "Partners in Crime" to go unspoiled. Moffat often requests that fans not post special showings on YouTube if they want previews to continue at Comic-Con. This has been successful with trailers for the 50th anniversary special and the behind-the-scenes docudrama *An Adventure in Space and Time.*

Amy's life with the Doctor is also characterized by books and words. She harnesses the power of storytelling, making it so powerful and filled with belief that she can drag the Doctor back from nonexistence, along with her family. Using River's journal as a touchstone, Amy summons the Doctor from her imagination into reality, just in time to dance at her wedding. For his part, the Doctor gathers up little Amelia and tells her his bedtime story of a box that's old and new, borrowed and blue. As he comments, "We're all stories in the end" ("The Big Bang"). When time stops in "The Wedding of River Song," Amy remembers her other life through her notes and artwork. "I have to keep doing this, writing and drawing things. It's just it's so hard to keep remembering."

In the entire Pandorica arc, the Doctor is caught in a trap made of Amy's childhood books and finally imprisoned inside Pandora's box, itself a work of mythology:

> DOCTOR: There was a goblin, or a trickster, or a warrior. A nameless, terrible thing, soaked in the blood of a billion galaxies. The most feared being in all the cosmos. And nothing could stop it, or hold it, or reason with it. One day it would just drop out of the sky and tear down your world.
> AMY: How did it end up in there?
> DOCTOR: You know fairy tales. A good wizard tricked it.
> RIVER: I hate good wizards in fairy tales. They always turn out to be him. ("The Pandorica Opens")

"It's a fairy tale, a legend. It can't be real," the Doctor protests. But as she points out earlier, River and the Doctor are stories as well, in their universe as well as in ours.

When Amy Pond criticizes the Time Lord bedtime story about the Shakri, the Eleventh Doctor replies, "You can talk. Wolf in your grandmother's night dress?" alluding to Little Red Riding Hood ("The Power of Three") Time Lord fairytales (which invariably come to life) appear in several adventures as the Shakri are supposedly "The pest controllers of the universe." The Doctor grew up with stories of the Toclafane, which the Master recreates in "The Sound of Drums." The Eleventh Doctor also humorously mentions his childhood favorites:

31

> Reading's great. You like stories, George? Yeah? Me, too.
> When I was your age, about, ooo, a thousand years ago, I
> loved a good bedtime story. The Three Little Sontarans.
> The Emperor Dalek's New Clothes. Snow White and the
> Seven Keys To Doomsday, eh? All the classics. ("Night
> Terrors")

Steven Moffat's very first *Doctor Who* story, published in 1996 in the anthology *Decalog 3,* is called "Continuity Errors." It takes place in a giant library, possibly the one of his episode "Silence in the Library." There, companion Bernice Summerfield tries to read the finished version of her own published diary, while the Doctor needs a book to end a war and save lives. When the librarian is unfriendly, the Doctor starts manipulating her past (similar to his actions in "A Christmas Carol") but her present fills with "continuity errors." Eventually, the Doctor succeeds and the book he wanted changes from *Massacre on Deltherus 5* to *Miracle on Deltherus 5*. This story is interspersed with a Lunar University lecture that deconstructs the Doctor, discussing how he's a terrible danger who snatches young women from their own timelines, brainwashes them, and then leaves them behind again. Apparently, his most insidious tactic is to insert himself into the popular fiction and even make up a TV show about himself so no one will believe he's real (a comment presented in a fictional work about fiction that could make readers' heads spin).

The Land of Fiction appeared in the Second Doctor serial, "The Mind Robber." The Master of the Land tries to convert companions Jamie and Zoe into his characters, in a fun self-referential twist. "The concept for 'The Mind Robber' came from an observation by Peter Ling, co-creator of *Crossroads,* observing that some *Doctor Who* fans seemed to believe that their favourite fictional characters were real," the BBC commentary on the episode notes (Martin). The Doctor chats with Gulliver from *Gulliver's Travels* (who only speaks using quotes from his novel), emphasizing their shared role as fictional travelers to unseen magical lands. Cyrano de Bergerac and Sir Lancelot fight beside the Doctor against illusory villains. As they wander, Zoe and the Doctor repeat to themselves that what they are seeing doesn't really exist – it's imaginary. Jaime reads his own story typed out in front of him like a script, and our heroes stumble through a forest of words before nearly getting crushed into the pages of a book. All this teases readers with the characters' fictional nature. The episode has a surreal quality, as they aren't clearly seen entering the Land of Fiction or leaving it – perhaps as fictional characters, they never do. The Sixth Doctor returns to the Land of Fiction in audio episodes and the Seventh Doctor visits in novelizations – it's a truly beloved area of the Doctor's universe.

In "The Professor, the Queen, and the Bookshop," Young Amelia and Young Rory stumble into a bookshop managed by the Doctor. The books there are named for *Who* stories that were set aside: *Shylock, Scratchman, The Dark Dimension, The Master of Luxor, The Song of the Space Whale, The Imps.* Amy even picks up a copy of the "lost episode" *Shada*. However, the Doctor cautions them that the library "moves," as they can travel into any world through the pages – a popular description of reading itself as well as a reminder of the TARDIS. The name of the place, Phoenix Books, references resurrection and eternal life, while the entrance and sign are TARDIS blue and the interior is seemingly infinite. They race through magical worlds, avoiding the terrible White Queen who made it "always winter and never Christmas" in a direct Narnia reference. As they encounter *Who* monsters within the pages, Amy literally fights using the power of books, and rewrites their story to save the Doctor. In the end, C.S. Lewis adapts their adventure into his famous *Chronicles of Narnia*, and the Inklings' newest member, the Doctor, suggests adding a magical wardrobe.

"The Shakespeare Code" is very much a story about the power of words. The theater itself, as a place of make-believe, becomes a source of another reality, just as the television set does.

> DOCTOR: Oh yeah, but a theatre's magic, isn't it? You should know. Stand on this stage, say the right words with the right emphasis a the right time. Oh, you can make men

33

weep, or cry with joy. Change them. You can change people's minds just with words in this place. But if you exaggerate that.
MARTHA: It's like your police box. Small wooden box with all that power inside.

The Doctor realizes that the play is a way of literally reshaping the world as well as figuratively. "Love's Labours Won. It's a weapon. The right combination of words, spoken at the right place, with the shape of the Globe as an energy converter! The play's the thing!" The Doctor tells Shakespeare that as the Carrionites are witches who use words to remake the world, Shakespeare can save everyone using the same tools: "Trust yourself. When you're locked away in your room, the words just come, don't they, like magic. Words of the right sound, the right shape, the right rhythm. Words that last forever. That's what you do, Will. You choose perfect words. Do it. Improvise." The Carrionites are chased off in a flurry of pages.

Other Who creators reach out to their favorite authors or even critics – In 1988's episode "Dragonfire," the Seventh Doctor and a guard debate the concept that "The semiotic thickness of a performed text varies according to the redundancy of its auxiliary performance codes." This is an actual quote from the academic book *Doctor Who: The Unfolding Text*, and simplified means "The less relevant an in-joke is to the plot, the more cultural significance it has" in a brief self-referential joke. In "Vincent and the Doctor," Dr. Black – Bill Nighy's character – explains to Van Gogh how the latter managed to "transform the pain of his tormented life into ecstatic beauty" and "use [his] passion and pain to portray the joy and ecstasy and magnificence of our world." Fans and reviewers spend their time making many similar comments on the show.

According to the Fourth Doctor novel *Managra,* a cult on Gallifrey celebrated a ritual called Thirteenth Night, combining it with the form of theatre called Mimesis, which allows the user to rewrite reality. The 31st century planet Managra (an anagram for anagram) uses this technology to bring fears and tales to life. Francis Pearson, a Shakespeare-era playwright transported to the planet, unites with the planet, becoming the composite entity Persona (an anagram of his name) and adopts the name Doctor Sperano (another anagram of Pearson and likely reference to Shakespeare's Prospero) and becomes the Dramaturge, director of the world. The Doctor and Sarah Jane must face him on his new world, surrounded by fictional characters and famous authors alike. They meet Mary and Percy Shelley, Alistair Crowley, Paracelsus, Johann Faust, multiple Cyrano de Bergeracs, Casanovas, Byrons, Marquis de Sades, Emily Brontes, Goethes, Mozarts, Beethovens, Tchaikovskys, Metternichs, Leonardo da Vincis, and the Four Musketeers.

> The Doctor was the finest dream of hundreds of human beings, refined as they tapped away at their typewriters. For generations, they'd made him a hero to countless millions in over a hundred countries. Then, just once, he hadn't come back. His enemies had kept him away. But despite their best efforts he hadn't been forgotten. There were those who remembered him when they walked past a dummy in a shop window or sat on a beach looking out to sea, and every time they ground pepper. Some of those who remembered him had typewriters of their own. And, after far too long, a new generation of children were about to hear that music for the first time, and they would learn their sofa wasn't just for sitting on. (Parkin)

The novel *The Gallifrey Chronicles* by Lance Parkin is a book about books and the Doctor. Marnal, the former Castellan of Gallifrey, is exiled to Earth in 1883, and there he writes numerous science fiction and fantasy novels, which actually contain the entire history of Gallifrey: *The Kraglon Inheritance, The Witch Lords, The Emergents, The Giants, The Hand of Time* (published in 1976), *The Time of Neman, The Beautiful People, Marnal's Journeys or the Modern Crusoe, Day of Wrath, The Monkey to Time* saga, and *Valley of the Lost*. He once wrote an episode of *Star Trek,* but it was changed so much that he refused credit. After Marnal dies, the Doctor collects and keeps all of his novels, preserving another history of Gallifrey. The Doctor tells his companion, "One of the things you'll learn is that it's all real.

35

Every word of every novel is real, every frame of every movie, every panel of every comic strip" prompting the self-critical reply, "But that's just not possible. I mean some books contradict other ones." This is a natural state of affiars in the Expanded Whoniverse.

"The Rings of Akhaten" is absolutely a story about the power of story. The Doctor explains that "The soul's made of stories, not atoms. Everything that ever happened to us," thus the people of Akhaten, especially their god-monster, are drawn to them and use them as currency. To save the young queen from sacrificing herself, the Doctor reaches out to her with his greatest strength:

> Hey, do you mind if I tell you a story? One you might not have heard. All the elements in your body were forged many, many millions of years ago, in the heart of a far away star that exploded and died. That explosion scattered those elements across the desolations of deep space. After so, so many millions of years, these elements came together to form new stars and new planets. And on and on it went. The elements came together and burst apart, forming shoes and ships and sealing wax, and cabbages and kings. Until eventually, they came together to make you. You are unique in the universe. There is only one Merry Gejelh. And there will never be another. Getting rid of that existence isn't a sacrifice. It is a waste. ("The Rings of Akhaten")

Queen Merry in fact leads them to their escape through her knowledge of legends, especially those of secret passages. Clara battles with the strength of her history and her talisman of a leaf – "full of stories, full of history. And full of a future that never got lived. Days that should have been that never were." The Doctor too defeats the creature by telling it a story – the story of itself and how it's a parasite that viscously consumes others to sustain its life. He ends his tale with a final story – the story of himself.

> So, come on, then. Take mine. Take my memories. But I hope you've got a big appetite, because I have lived a long life and I have seen a few things. I walked away from the

36

last Great Time War. I marked the passing of the Time Lords. I saw the birth of the universe and I watched as time ran out, moment by moment, until nothing remained. No time. No space. Just me. I walked in universes where the laws of physics were devised by the mind of a mad man. I've watched universes freeze and creations burn. I've seen things you wouldn't believe. I have lost things you will never understand. And I know things. Secrets that must never be told. Knowledge that must never be spoken. Knowledge that will make parasite gods blaze. So come on, then. Take it! Take it all, baby! Have it! You have it all! ("The Rings of Akhaten")

In *Wolfsbane,* a novel by Jacqueline Rayner, the Eighth Doctor, still suffering from amnesia, submits short stories from his adventures to classic science fiction magazine *Astounding Stories,* just as many *Who* writers once did. These include the Cybermen, the clockwork soldiers of "The Mind Robber," walking cacti (presumably Meglos), the Axons (from "The Claws of Axos"), and the lost city of Atlantis (visited in "The Underwater Menace" and "The Time Monster." In the short story "Mordieu," the Eighth Doctor tries writing in the 1960s for American television, while in "The Kingmaker," the Doctor mentions that he wrote a series of children's books during his adventures with UNIT in the seventies.

The Companions too become writers on their adventures. Sarah Jane Smith wrote the book *UNIT: Fighting for Humankind* (seen in "Whatever Happened to Sarah Jane?"). Amelia Williams apparently became an author and wrote *Summer Falls* in the past. Clara sees her young charge reading it in "The Bells of Saint John," and tells him that chapter ten is good but "eleven is the best. You'll cry your eyes out." In an extra-fannish moment, the contrast between the tenth and eleventh is likely a reference to the Tenth and Eleventh Doctors and their warring popularity. *Summer Falls* was made into an actual digital novel by the BBC and released April 4th, 2013, bringing the fictional moment to life.

"The Angels Take Manhattan" opens with a clicking typewriter and the narration of a Raymond Chandler detective story. Once again, readers are reminded they're watching fiction. The Doctor is reading the novel aloud, a tale of Melody Malone, who has "ice in her heart and a kiss on her lips, and a vulnerable side she keeps well hidden."

"Only you could fancy someone in a book," Rory tells the Doctor. In fact, Melody Malone is actually River Song and Rory is transported back in time and thus into the novel:

> Doctor: (reads) I followed the skinny guy for two more blocks before he turned and I could ask exactly what he was doing here. He looked a little scared, so I gave him my best smile and my bluest eyes.
> Amy: [...] Doctor? What did the skinny guy say?
> Doctor: He said, "I just went to get coffees for the Doctor and Amy. Hello, River." ("The Angels Take Manhattan")

The Doctor and Amy must solve the mystery in the book and in their own lives, reading ahead without spoiling as whatever Amy reads will then come true.

> Amy: Time can be rewritten.
> Doctor: Not once you've read it. Once we know what's coming, it's written in stone. ("The Angels Take Manhattan")

There's a cut to a nearby gravestone inscribed "In Loving Memory Rory Arthur Williams," indeed read and written in stone (though by the audience not the characters). The Melody Malone book finally offers both Doctor and readers Amy's final goodbye: Amy's final request is that the Doctor find the younger her and "tell her a story...Tell her this is the story of Amelia Pond. And this how it ends" ("The Angels Take Manhattan"). In 2012, BBC Books released the ebook *The Angel's Kiss: A Melody Malone Story*, a prequel to the book that the Doctor was reading in the episode, in another moment of fiction becoming reality.

Troubles with the Idiot's Lantern

Earlier in Russell Davies' career, between 1988 and 1992, he produced the television show *Why Don't You?* which pushed children to stop watching television and do something constructive (a complex, circular message for a television program). As one critic notes, "The minor hypocrisy of the message – "Thanks for watching my television show, now stop watching television" – has followed Davies into his career on Doctor Who," Marc Edward DiPaolo explains in "Political Satire and British-American Relations in Five Decades of *Doctor Who*" (972).

Indeed, the Doctor delights in books, but also warns against the dangers of internet and television addiction. As critic Sue Short notes, many episodes question media power, including "Bad Wolf," the show about killer gameshows and "Love and Monsters," which stars the Absorbaloff – "a monstrous depiction of avaricious fandom literally living off other people" (175). Killer cellphone earpieces and idiot news channels satirize much of our modern culture. The creatures of the Silence are killed because they send out a message on television for the human race to defend itself. Viewers along with the people of 1969 see "You should kill us all on sight!" which then becomes a post-hypnotic suggestion to the entire human race. As Elaine Graham notes in her book on the monstrous, "representations of the post/human" in the "'stories we live by' can be important critical tools in the task of articulating what it means to be human in a digital and bio-technological age" (17).

In the first episode of the reboot, "Rose," the Ninth Doctor (Christopher Eccleston) criticizes Rose Tyler (Billie Piper), for being a typical human. "I mean, you lot, all you do is eat chips, go to bed and watch telly, while all the time underneath you there's a war going on!" ("Rose"). The episode's monsters, Autons, are plastic aliens, and "plastic is a distinctly corporate product that frequently symbolizes all that is wrong with our current culture of mass-consumption" (Schuster and Powers 122). Rose Tyler, in contrast, appears to represent "The desire to

39

live as more than just a mindless consumer" (Schuster and Powers 123). Of course, she leaves earth and her telly to join him in the battle.

Likewise, Rose's friend Adam accompanies her and the Ninth Doctor into the future in "The Long Game." "He becomes a negative example and a condemnation of those who cannot stop immersing themselves in television, the Internet, iPods, and other nonstop broadcasters of what the Doctor calls 'useless information'" (DiPaolo 972-973). In the future, he buys a cybernetic implant that lets him download unlimited information, which he's incapable of absorbing. The information fills his head, but he has no understanding of it and certainly no deeper wisdom as he only wants to use it for profit. The disgusted Ninth Doctor drops him back on earth to live with the consequences. As DiPaolo adds:

> The joke is on Adam because all of the information he downloaded into his brain was controlled, censored, and rewritten by the Jagrafess, a loathsome alien being clearly intended to represent mass media mogul Rupert Murdoch, owner of, among other things, *The New York Post*, *The Sun*, *Star Magazine*, 20th Century Fox, Fox News, *The Wall Street Journal*, Harper Collins, IGN Entertainment, and MySpace. Thus, all Adam succeeds in doing is becoming a spy and a stooge for the Jagrafess. (972-973)

"Satellite Five and the Game Station render humanity as susceptible to becoming mindless consumers of commodities and useless information as do our own mass-media outlets on present-day earth" Schuster and Powers note in *The Greatest Show in the Galaxy,* their book on *Doctor Who* as cultural statement (124). Visiting Satellite Five later, the Doctor calls humanity "Brainless sheep" for watching reality TV, but reveals he enjoys it as well, asking, "Mind you, have they still got that program where three people have to live with a bear?" ("Bad Wolf"). In this episode, the television has turned murderous, as contestants are shot on *The Weakest Link* and permanently eradicated on *Big Brother*. As Lynda-with-a-Y explains, "There's *Call My Bluff,* with real guns. *Countdown,* where you've got thirty seconds to stop the bomb going off. *Ground Force*, which is a nasty one. You get turned into compost. Er, *Wipeout*, speaks for itself. Oh, and *Stars In Their Eyes*. Literally, stars in their eyes. If you don't sing, you get blinded" ("Bad Wolf"). All of these are actual UK reality shows, subtly emphasizing the harm inherent in this type of exploitation.

"You lot, you're obsessed. You'd do anything for the latest upgrade," the Doctor notes in "Rise of the Cybermen." In fact, the prized cellphone earpieces on Pete's World become the key to controlling the population, then converting them into Cybermen in a literal "upgrade" – a warning about the hazards of an overly technological world. The Cybermen note, "We have been upgraded [into] the next level of mankind. We are Human point two. Every citizen will receive a free upgrade. You will become like us" ("Rise of the Cybermen"), chillingly our own catchphrases. The robot-like humans who tune in to music, news, and other media become literal robots as they disconnect from society. Cybus Industries with its madman CEO John Lumic offers Cybus earbuds (even diamond-studded ones!) and their Daily Download of lottery numbers and jokes, which hypnotize their eager consumers as much as texts and emails do on smartphones today. The Cybus logo actually resembles a computer's power button, turned sideways. "A logo on the front," the Doctor notes. "Lumic's turned it into a brand." This works as both commercial branding and a slave's brand of ownership – one in some ways equals the other.

> "Rise of the Cybermen" and "The Age of Steel" (both 2006),suggest that society's fascination for new and improved technology can be of a benefit to the continued evolution of humanity – The Doctor comments on the ingenuity of the human race in creating gadgets and gizmos such as mobile phones and Bluetooth headsets that entertain and enrich lives. It is only when humans – and in particular the Cybus Industries owner, John Lumic – become paranoid about the fragile nature of the organic body that they start to look to the potentials of the Cyber-race and their metal bodies. (Geraghty 95).

On "The Idiot's Lantern," the television is spreading through post-war Britain, turning avid watchers into "monsters." Their faces vanish and their souls are wiped of everything — a metaphor for television where loved ones no longer see the person's face and their heads are filled with empty nonsense. The television monster "The Wire" is endlessly hungry and slurps away at people even as they struggle. The Tenth Doctor (David Tennant) notes, "It feeds off the electrical activity of the brain, but it gorges itself like a great overfed pig, taking people's faces, their essences. It stuffs itself" ("The Idiot's Lantern"). Her slave, metaphorically a slave to the television, says he only craves "peace," away from her. Thus the new *Doctor Who* offers "an extended riff on advertising, consumerism, and the entertainment industry" (Schuster and Powers 119). Of course, the episode's title in the first place points out television's dumbed-down, moth-to-a-flame appeal.

There had been several recent reports of SatNav devices giving drivers incorrect information, leading to accidents and even near-fatalities, so the ATMOS device was created for "The Sontaran Strategem." Along with the horror of technology and the environmental message, there's a subtle protest at people who would follow driving directions straight into the ocean, directed by their shiny new satellite navigation system. This is also spoofed with the Victorian child "Thomas Thomas" who gives directions in "The Crimson Horror."

On *Torchwood's* "From Out of the Rain," movies are the terrible threat, as the Night Travelers are preserved on ancient filmstrips. When a film is shown, they are freed to travel the world and steal victims' breaths. The Torchwood team refilm them and expose the film to sunlight, destroying them. Jack Harkness claims that they can come back from other old film canisters, as happens at episode end.

"Revelation of the Daleks" shows two applications of audio-visual systems. One is given in the free-spirited and jocose VJ, who mixes popular music, images from the surrounding environment, and his own patter for entertainment purposes. The other is given in Davros, the evil geneticist

who monitors all that goes on in Tranquil Repose, the
funerary and cryonic establishment he has taken over in
order to carry out his experiments. The two characters are
linked as thematic oppo5sites: both have access to the
same audio-visual system. (Layton, "Closed Circuits" 243)

When they're introduced, V.J. and Davros are watching the
same event – the arrival of the Sixth Doctor (Colin Baker) and
his companion Peri (Nicola Bryant). VJ interprets events, calling
Peri "a maiden in distress" and acts, in some ways like a sports
commentator or DVD commentary. He's a corpulent couch
potato, like his television audience – one of them, in fact. With
phrases such as, "Hey guys, viddy this!" or "I'll be hearing from
you, all right?" he calls for participation from his friends, and by
extension from the audience. When his life is threatened, the VJ
turns the system into a weapon, "a highly directional ultrasonic
beam of rock and roll. It kills!" The television becomes, not only
his identity, but his power. Peri, the American companion, is
likewise pleased and entertained by the television.

Davros by contrast controls the action, tricking the Doctor
into coming in the first place. His surveillance system ensures
that he can control the civilization, not just watch it. He's
determined to know more than anyone, as he repeatedly
executes people for "knowing too much." While he comments
on events, he also chooses what to do about them. "On the
other hand, his reliance on the audio-visual system is a
weakness, as is shown by his fear of someone using his name on
an open videophone channel. His image from the videophone is
used so that assassins can identify him. The system can even be
turned against him when the VJ and Peri use it to warn off the
President's ship from the dangers at Tranquil Repose" (Layton,
"Closed Circuits" 244).

"'Vengeance on Varos' examines the ways a government can
use television to control the populace and subdue subversion
and yet itself become slave to the audio-visual system. Of final
interest is the way that in *Doctor Who* TV explores its own
dangers and limitations" (Layton, "Closed Circuits" 242-243).
Etta and Arak are a couple who spend the episode observing –

43

they are the show's "ordinary viewers." They begin the show watching an execution, mindlessly enjoying the same violence seen on "Bad Wolf" (and on *The Hunger Games,* for that matter). "When did we last see a decent execution?" asks Arak. Eventually, the pair find themselves watching the Doctor's exploits (as the real viewers are), swept away with admiration for his heroism. The villain here is the legless slug Sil, the ultimate couch potato and exploiter of others. "TV also becomes for Etta and Arak the center of their personal political cosmos, pitting the dissatisfied Arak against the loyal Etta in a microcosmic battle in which a viewer's report becomes a major weapon. In their world, in which TV is the sole means of both information and entertainment and the only mediator between the two people, whoever controls that device controls them" (Layton, "Closed Circuits" 245). Giving up one's mind means others can exploit it, as mindless watchers trade free will for entertainment.

Clara Oswald (Jenna Coleman)'s first appearance in the twenty-first century, "The Bells of Saint John," could be termed a story of internet addiction. Moffat described the premise as "The traditional 'Doctor Who' thing of taking something omnipresent in your life and making it sinister, if something did get in the Wi-Fi, we'd be kind of screwed. Nobody had really done it before, so I thought, 'It's time to get kids frightened of Wi-Fi!'" (*Doctor Who Magazine* 458). Those who log onto the strange wireless internet connection are sucked into the computer and turned into literally hollow copies of themselves unable to do more than parrot their catchphrases. As the episode's exposition warns, "Their souls live on, trapped. Sometimes you can hear their cries, 'I don't know where I am,' on the radio, on the telly, or on the net." This appears to be a warning against internet addiction, as those who are preyed upon improve their skills with technology but are permanently trapped in tiny computer screens. Moffat however denied that his intention was to give a warning about technology, but rather tell an adventure story about a "new way [for aliens] to invade" based on something viewers were familiar with (Radish, "Matt

Smith"). However humorous, the story calls to attention how much the technology has permeated our society, emptying people's heads until they resemble the "spoonhead robots" in truth:

> DOCTOR: This whole world is swimming in wifi. We're living in a wifi soup. Suppose something got inside it. Suppose there was something living in the wifi, harvesting human minds. Extracting them. Imagine that. Human souls trapped like flies in the world-wide web. Stuck forever, crying out for help.
> CLARA: Isn't that basically Twitter? ("The Bells of Saint John")

The enemy is defeated because of their unthinking fondness for social media – another commentary on today's society:

> CLARA: You've hacked the lower operating system, yeah? I'll have their physical location in under five minutes. Pop off and get us a coffee.
> DOCTOR: If I can't find them, you definitely can't.
> CLARA: They uploaded me, remember? I've got computing stuff in my head....It's never about the security, it's about the people.
> …
> ALEXI: Someone's hacking the webcams. All of them.
> MAHLER: Everybody check your webcams.
> ALEXI: But what would be the point, taking mug shots of us?
> MAHLER: Who's on Facebook?
> Hands go up.
> MAHLER: Bebo? MySpace? Abo?
> More hands.
> MAHLER: Put your hands down if you didn't mention where you work.
> No hands go down. ("The Bells of Saint John")

"That moment, in which the villains are hoist with their own social media petard, offers the episode's most trenchant insight into the follies and fears of the Internet age" (Wilkins). In "The Power of Three" Smith puts disgust into the Doctor's remark concerning Twitter in the episode, reflecting his real-life decision to stay off the social network (Mulkern). Davies seems to share his feelings, commenting in 2007, "In the community of sci-fi shows, I think we're the only one that actively ignores its online fanbase. American shows seem to court them, or pretend that they do. That way lies madness. I cannot think of a show that's improved its quality, or its ratings, by doing it. It is like going in search of a massively biased focus group – why would anyone do that?" (qtd. in DiPaolo 975)

Likewise, in "Planet of the Dead," The UNIT automated helpline is so terrible it might doom the world to an alien invasion as the Doctor is put on hold:

> PHONE: This is the Unified Intelligence Taskforce. Please select one of the following four options. If you want to report a UFO sighting, press one...
> DOCTOR: Aw, I hate these things.

In a world of advertisements, television monsters, corrupting cellphones, and brain-sucking internet, it's important to keep things in perspective and not get overwhelmed. "Following the Doctor's cue, we'd do best to approach these corporations – and our own relationships to them – with critical minds. We must question the meaningless drivel of the advertising industry. We must recognize the power of corporate logos and slogans to invade our minds and spread among us like viruses," Schuster and Powers explain (135).

Breaking the Fourth Wall

> DOCTOR: Smile, Jo.
> JO: What?
> DOCTOR: You're on camera.
> The Doctor waves at the CCTV at the fortress prison they're visiting. ("The Mind of Evil")

Obviously such moments are amusing and reflective as the Third Doctor (Jon Pertwee) and his companion Jo Grant (Katy Manning) are on camera literally as well as fictionally. In "The

46

Mind of Evil," the Master watches the Doctor's nightmares of Daleks and monsters on a television screen of a sort, emphasizing the watchable and fictional nature of the Doctor's foes…even himself. In another scene, the Brigadier and his aid plot a break in.

> BRIGADIER: Have you seen Stangmoor Prison?
> COSWORTH: No, sir.
> BRIGADIER: Well, I've just been looking at it. It's an old fortress. You'd need an army to get in there.
> COSWORTH: A fortress?
> BRIGADIER: That's right.
> COSWORTH: I suppose there couldn't possible be a secret underground passage or something?
> BRIGADIER: Good, Major, good. Is that a map of the prison?
> COSWORTH: Yes, sir.
> BRIGADIER: Yes, you're right. It hasn't been blocked off either. It probably leads to the old dungeons.
> COSWORTH: It's rather like making a film, isn't it, sir. ("The Mind of Evil")

Even in the first episode, the Doctor points out the magic of our televised world when new companion Ian Chesterton (William Russell) is agape at the TARDIS, bigger on the inside.

> DOCTOR: But you've discovered television, haven't you?
> IAN: Yes.
> DOCTOR: Then by showing an enormous building on your television screen, you can do what seemed impossible, couldn't you? ("An Unearthly Child")

This delightful self-reference tells viewers they can enter a marvelous world simply through watching. Of course, the greatest self-references involve clips of past Doctors, reminding viewers of the past and how it blends with the future's canon.

When Davros taunts the Doctor in "Journey's End," he sees those who sacrificed themselves to save him from the beginning of the new series: Harriet Jones, Jabe, the Controller and Lynda from "Bad Wolf," Robert MacLeish from "Tooth and Claw,"

Mrs. Moore, the team of LINDA, the Face of Boe, Chantho the Master's assistant, Astrid Peth, Luke Rattigan, his daughter Jenny, River Song at her death, and the hostess of "Midnight." A second flashback sequence travels through all of Donna's adventures.

Travis Flickett of *IGN* describes the concept of "fan service," cute moments like these that amuse the fans rather than moving the story forward:

> The idea of "fan service" is always a double edged sword. It's great to see all of the things you may like about a series come together on screen, but it so often works better in theory than in practice. It's like those giant crossovers that comic books do all the time – where every cool character meets every other cool character. While it's interesting (to a degree) that they're sharing a page, everybody ends up getting short-shrift. (Flickett)

"The Stolen Earth"/"Journey's End" ends the Davies era with a bang as Sarah Jane (with her house, Mr. Smith, K-9, and Luke), Captain Jack (with Gwen , Ianto, and the Torchwood base), Rose, Donna, Martha, and their families all battle to save the world, aided by UNIT and Harriet Jones. They also journey to the frequently-mentioned Shadow Proclamation to face the highest arbiters of the universe law. This epic story was actually much more elaborate in its first draft: The Daleks were intended to invade earth in a shot of their saucers filling the sky, not just their voices on audio. One saucer would shatter Big Ben and shoot the Prime Minister in a callback to earlier invasions of London. The Shadow Proclamation, a city which arched over multiple asteroids with shining metal towers, originally featured all the aliens from *New Who* with a few particular cameos:

47: INT. Shadow Proclamation lobby: Night.
Close on the Doctor and Donna – who's recovering, brave face on – both stepping out...

The Doctor: ...right, the first thing we've got to do is...
Stops dead, as a platoon of Judoon march past, big, heavy
boots stomping, left to right, the Doctor and Donna nipping
through a gap in the formation, pushing forward...
The Doctor: ...whoops, 'scuse me, sorry...
FX: Three Krillitanes swoop down, the Doctor and Donna
brushing them off, still pushing forward...
Donna: Oy! Get off!
The Doctor: Keep your wings in, you lot!...then stopped by
two Vespiforms buzzing right to left...
The Doctor: ...oh, mind those stings, thank you...
The Doctor and Donna then stopping to look properly. Gulp.
FX: Wide shot. Big, white open smart-sci-fi-building. Filled
with crowd multiplication Judoon, crowd multiplication
Slitheen, a few Hath, two helmeted Sycorax, and crowd
multiplication space-extras: some in big opera cloaks;
Sisters of the Wicker Place Mat from 1.2; plus a lot of
monks and nuns. Also, Shadow police: like Judoon, but
Human, in big stompy black uniforms. Flying through the
air: Krillitanes; Vespiforms; and Gelth. And in one corner, a
huge 15ft Adipose, mewling. All busy, chaotic, emergency!
The Doctor: Tell me, what's everyone doing here?
Slitheen: The whole universe is on red alert! Planets have
disappeared! We have lost Clom!
The Doctor: Clom's gone?!
Slitheen: Clom's gone!
Donna: What's Clom?
Slitheen: Our twin planet! Without it,
Raxacoricofallapatorius will fall out of the sky! [turns to
go] We must phone home... [to Baby Slitheen] ...this way,
Margaret.
Baby Slitheen talks with the voice of Margaret Blaine:
Baby Slitheen: Take me home, Daddy, I don't like the nasty
policemen! (Davies & Cook 345)

"Is this world protected?" the Doctor demands in "The
Eleventh Hour." Images flash through the Atraxi's projection:
Cybermen, The Daleks spitting outward from the Genesis Ark.
The Empress of the Racnoss. The Ood. The Sycorax. The
Sontarans. The Silurians The Reapers. The Hath. "Cause you're
not the first lot to have come here. Oh, there have been so
many. And what you've got to ask is... what happened to them?"

49

He steps through shots of all the first ten Doctors in order, then steps through them to make the Eleventh. "Hello. I'm the Doctor. Basically...run."

In "The Almost People," the Doctor's Ganger mumbles, "one day we will get back" from "An Unearthly Child," uses the Third Doctor's catchphrase "reverse the polarity of the neutron flow," craves the Fourth Doctor's jelly babies, and mimics the Tenth Doctor. An unfortunately cut scene would have included a montage of the Doctor's happy memories, including old and new episodes as well as events that had not transpired onscreen (Hickman 80).

In "Journey to the Centre of the Tardis," the TARDIS leaks famous moments out of the past, quoting the first episode, "An Unearthly Child," as well as recent companions Rose, Martha, and Amy on their first adventures. The Eleventh Doctor calls the TARDIS sexy, and early companion Susan Foreman (Carole Ann Ford) explains how she made up the name from the initials: Time and Relative Dimension In Space" ("An Unearthly Child"). The Third and Fourth Doctors chime in as well, as the Third prattles to Jo about daisies and the Fourth contemplates the genocide of the Daleks. The Sixth Doctor warns the Time Lords, "Daleks, Sontarans, Cybermen! They're still in the nursery compared to us," during his trial on Gallifrey.

"The Name of the Doctor" offers many clips—original, restaged by recent actors, and even colorized in the first *Doctor Who* example yet. The scene of the First Doctor stealing the TARDIS (not yet a police box) is also shown for the first time. Traveling back into all their episodes, Clara saves him by cautioning him to steal the proper Type 40 one, and then calls after the Third Doctor in Bessie and the Second in his fur coat (both in scenes from "The Five Doctors"). Clara aids the Fourth Doctor in "The Invasion of Time," the Fifth in "Arc of Infinity," and the Tenth in "Silence in the Library," while she watches the Seventh dangle off a cliff by his umbrella in "Dragonfire."

In several episodes, the Doctor delights fans by addressing remarks to the camera: On "The Snowmen," the Eleventh

Doctor's final line, "Watch me run," is delivered right to the audience. They indeed get to watch him run as the second half of series seven begins a search for Clara and new purpose for the Doctor and his fans alike. In "The Curse of the Black Spot" he stares at the camera. "Feels like something's out there...staring straight at me." Obviously, there is. The Tenth Doctor (David Tennant) interacts with the audience more directly when encouraging them to applaud louder and showering the orchestra with the pages he's written in his 2008 BBC Proms Season video appearance – he's said to be using a space portal from the TARDIS to the Royal Albert Hall.

Meanwhile, an episode titled Doctor Who: "The Greatest Show in the Galaxy" must be considered at least a bit self-referential. In the episode, the Seventh Doctor (Sylvester McCoy) performs in the circus, emphasizing his role as performer on his television episodes. As he talks with Morgana, who can see the future in a different way than he can, the Doctor faces his role as simultaneous performer and traveler.

> DOCTOR: The Psychic Circus has grown into quite a sizeable operation, by the looks of it.
> MORGANA: The greatest show in the galaxy.
> DOCTOR: Quite so, yes. My, you have travelled, haven't you? The planet Othris, the Boriatic Wastes, Marpesia and the Grand Pagoda of Cinethon.
> MORGANA: Yes, we used to have a great time in the old days, going from planet to planet. But we've really got settled in here since
> DOCTOR: Since?
> MORGANA: Well, you have to hang up your travelling shoes and stop wandering sooner or later, don't you?
> DOCTOR: So I've been told. Personally, I just keep on wandering.

The episode opens like a curtain going up on a performance as the Ringmaster promises a delightful family show, much like *Doctor Who* itself: The Ringmaster promises "acts that are cool and acts that amaze," adding, "There are lots of surprises for the family at the Greatest Show in the Galaxy! So many strange surprises, I'm prepared to bet, whatever you've seen before, you ain't seen nothing yet." The audience is a stand-in for us, the television viewing audience, as the Doctor engages with them and they begin criticizing:

> DAD: You are trifling with us.
> DOCTOR: Really? I thought I was entertaining you.
> DAD: You are on the brink of destruction, Doctor. We want something bigger, something better.
> DOCTOR: Do you now?

He's voicing the home audience's desire for more, better, grander. "It was your show all along, wasn't it?" his companion Ace (Sophie Aldred) acknowledges at the end. Indeed, the Doctor rules the circus and the larger show beyond. Thus his role as entertainer comes into prominence.

The acknowledgement that they're all on television is always an excuse for fun. In "Night Terrors," a parent worries his child has been watching too much scary television and needs to shut it off. The Doctor emphatically replies that he shouldn't do *that*... Madame Kovarian peeks out of a pale square in *The Brilliant Book 2012* and speaks as herself, in another disturbingly believable moment. Finally, one of the old series' last episodes has a delightful moment as someone on television within the show announces, "This is BBC television. The time is a quarter past five and Saturday viewing continues with an adventure in the new science fiction series, Doc–" ("Remembrance of the Daleks"). By thus winking at viewers, the Doctor builds a larger world, dragging his fans into his fictional show and inviting them to interact there.

How We See Ourselves: Fan Episodes

DOCTOR: "A science geek?" What's that mean?
MARTHA: Means you're obsessively enthusiastic about it.
DOCTOR: (happily) Oh, okay! ("The Lazarus Experiment")

Several *New Who* episodes, beginning with "Rose," show science fiction fans integral to the plot. Searching for the Ninth Doctor (Christopher Eccleston), Rose Tyler (Billie Piper) approaches the couch potato Clive, who's been tracking the Doctor and gathering witnesses over the internet. Clive's family is unappreciative of his search for the Doctor, as his son greets Rose with "Dad! It's one of your nutters!" His wife is surprised Rose is female…and again, *Doctor Who* fandom and science fiction fandom were famously male for many years. Clive keeps a shed as a private den of fandom, where he pursues his not-so-ridiculous theory the Doctor is an alien from another world. He explores online, reading "Political diaries, conspiracy theories, even ghost stories." When Rose listens to his teachings, she too is inducted into the world of fandom.

In fact, a world of fans have had fifty years to create stories for their hero and his companions, old and new: Target produced novelizations of the original episodes in the 70s and 80s (the five that weren't done were unofficially finished off by the New Zealand Doctor Who Fan Club). Target also added a brief series called The Companions of Doctor Who. The Doctor Who New Adventures, also called the Virgin New Adventures, continued the travels of the Seventh Doctor and Ace after the original series ended, while Doctor Who Missing Adventures created new stories for the old Doctors. BBC published the Eighth Doctor Adventures, giving him many new companions and brought out their own Past Doctor Adventures. Spinoff novels included Faction Paradox, Bernice Summerfield, and Iris Wildthyme as original characters went on giant adventures in the official or often unofficial Whoniverse. The New Series Adventures are *New Who* books aimed at kids, while for the Fiftieth Anniversary, Puffin ebooks is releasing eleven authors' short stories for the eleven Doctors.

Big Finish audios, from 1999 onwards, include the New Eighth Doctor Adventures as well as various series within the larger universe such as The Companion Chronicles, Short Trips, Unbound, Gallifrey, UNIT, and so forth. BBC Audio has also made original audio books and audio versions of existing novels, once more featuring some of the original TV actors. Tom Baker also recorded some audio plays for BBC Audio. BBC Audio/AudioGO and Big Finish are finally uniting for the 50th anniversary series "Destiny of the Doctor."

Various comics including *Doctor Who* and *The Dalek Chronicles* ran in the sixties. In 1979, *Doctor Who Magazine* was created, with original comics that have branched off into their own universe of internal consistency and continue to come out through today. *New Who* was accompanied by the kids' magazine *Doctor Who Adventures,* with its own comics. The American IDW Comics produces comic books and graphic novels, including a *Star Trek* crossover.

There are choose-your-own-adventure style books for the Sixth, Tenth and Eleventh Doctors. Stage plays and musical include *The Curse of the Daleks, Doctor Who and The Daleks in the Seven Keys to Doomsday,* and *Doctor Who: The Ultimate Adventure.* There are licensed computer games called the Adventure Games series, tied to the Amy, Rory, and Eleventh Doctor era (Previously there was *Destiny of the Doctors* in the late 1990s). There are three licensed role playing games, from the nineties through recent times as well as the online *Doctor Who: Worlds in Time.*

Original cartoons available on DVD include *Death Comes to Time* (which kills the Doctor), *Shada* (with the Eighth Doctor replacing the Fourth), *Real Time* (joining Sixth Doctor actor Colin Baker and Big Finish companion Evelyn), *Scream of the Shalka* (with a new Doctor), *The Infinite Quest* (starring Tennant and Martha), and *Dreamland* (starring Tennant and temporary companions).

Of course, the productions are going in two directions, originating from fans as much as from the hired producers and authors. Henry Jenkins, author of the definitive work on fandom, *Textual Poachers,* explains that *Harry Potter* fandom pioneered the use of the web to create enormous teen communities in a way other fandoms like *Doctor Who* are still using today:

> The experience of reading, debating, performing, and rewriting Harry Potter has been shared by many in the millennial generation. Emerging alongside the popular embrace of the Web, Harry Potter fandom has developed new media platforms and practices. The community was among the first to use podcasting and blogs, to develop beta reading practices to improve fan fiction, to distribute mp3 files (such as those of Wizard Rock) through social networking sites, and to use machinima production practices to construct fan vids. (qtd. in Frankel 39)

Today, teen *Doctor Who* fans are following suit by creating fan videos and fanfiction. Review blogs and podcasts chart the Doctor's latest actions and speculate on the future. eBay and Etsy are filled with TARDIS and Dalek dresses, adipose earrings, bow tie hairbows, and decorated cellphone cases. Bibs sport the slogan "Bibs are Cool." People create TARDIS sheds and bookshelves and trendy "Keep Calm" slogans like "Keep Calm and Wear a Bow Tie" or "Keep Calm and Basically…Run." Time Lord Rock (inspired by Wizard Rock) has bands performing songs about their heroes for download by other fans or at conventions and concerts. There's an entire world out there of Pintrest memes and Facebook groups where fans post fun art and projects.

Creators as Fans

Why has the revived *Doctor Who* been so successful? One word: love. First of all, the BBC allowed the TARDIS to be taken over by Who-adoring fans Davies and Moffat. "*Doctor Who* used to be a show made by people who didn't necessarily love it," says the latter. "Some did – Tom Baker did. But it was a workaday show. Everybody who works at *Doctor Who* now is a devotee, somebody who grew up loving it. We regard it as a sacred trust" (Collis, "Doctor Who?"). If "the difference between watching a series and becoming a fan lies in the intensity of their emotional and intellectual involvement," the ones behind *New Who* aren't just creators – they're devotees (Jenkins 56).

"Certain now-influential figures have made the transition from hobbyist to paid expert, including Paul Cornell, Nicholas Briggs, Russell T Davies, Steven Moffat, and David Tennant. This invariably complicates the definition of what it means to be a fan" (Britton 58). Davies wrote the Virgin New Adventures novel *Damaged Goods,* and Moffat wrote short stories. "The Lodger" was loosely based on Gareth Roberts's comic strip by that name, published in *Doctor Who Magazine* in 2007.

Though licensed, these all took on qualities on fanfiction. Fanfiction traditionally involves rewriting characters and possibly "shipping" them—creating experimental romances unseen in the original. Emotions are usually higher in the fanfiction, and endings tacked on to existing scenes and episodes are a popular pastime as well. However, Davies and Moffat do these practices as well, as Davies creates a way for Rose to settle down with a Doctor *and* for the Tenth Doctor to keep adventuring, or the Eleventh Doctor and River can each rewrite the scene at Lake Silencio until they find a better conclusion. The Moffat era featured numerous extra scenes found on YouTube and DVD extras, showing River and the Doctor's first date or the scene after Amy tries to seduce the Doctor. Finally, the Tenth and Eleventh Doctors are far more emotional and relationship-oriented than the first seven Doctors put together.

Several moments caught between fanfiction and official

productions likewise muddy the distinction. In the Special Features section of "Earthshock's" *DVD*, there's a Claymation parody in which Adric is eaten by a dinosaur. "Pyramids of Mars," "City of Death," and "The Green Death" feature mockumentaries. David Tennant stars in a parody video as a companion in a long blonde wig. Davies had even hoped to write crossover fiction with *Star Trek: Enterprise,* as he explains in *The Writer's Tale.* Thus the creators mimic fanfiction writers, and indeed, were authors of the noncanon fanfiction and novelizations before becoming showrunners and scriptwriters, the most canon-centric "insiders" of all.

Slash fanfiction involves a same-sex romantic relationship – generally characters not in a relationship in the original text, like Harry and Draco or the Tenth Doctor and the Master. The term originated around the 1970s in the *Star Trek* fandom, with the popular Kirk/Spock pairing. Jenkins explains that slash "represents a reaction against the construction of male sexuality on television and in pornography," and invites readers "to imagine something akin to the liberating transgression of gender hierarchy" (189). Thus fanfiction becomes subversive, tearing down traditional gender roles or the ancient unspoken rule of "no hanky-panky in the TARDIS."

However, having the creators write the slash removes much of the subversion…at least on the surface. Moffat's "The Doctor Dances" feels remarkably like fanfiction as Jack Harkness, the first homosexual or perhaps pansexual companion, seduces everyone on screen and the Doctor seems offended that Rose assumes he's asexual (a theory that writers of the first seven Doctors seem to have established).

In Moffat's era there are many casual mentions of married gay couples, especially the beloved Madame Vastra and Jenny, "her suspiciously intimate companion," as Doctor Simeon calls her.

Vastra calmly retorts, "I resent your implication of impropriety. We are married" ("The Snowmen"). Vastra and Jenny too seem like fanfiction characters, not only for their gender subversion but their power as they, the minor characters, frankly take over an episode. They are two independent women operating in Victorian culture – one of the most infantilizing time periods for women. Jenkins adds that slash confronts "the most repressive forms of sexual identity" and provides "utopian alternatives to current configurations of gender" (189). This is their pairing in a nutshell.

The Doctor as Fan

One of the greatest literary fans of all appears to be the Doctor himself. In "The Unquiet Dead," the Doctor is thrilled to have abducted Charles Dickens. He calls him brilliant and gushes over *Great Expectations, Oliver Twist,* and "The Signal Man." Dickens is used to admiration but it seems the word fan hasn't been invented yet:

> DOCTOR: Honestly, Charles. Can I call you Charles? I'm such a big fan.
> DICKENS: A what? A big what?
> DOCTOR: Fan. Number one fan, that's me.
> DICKENS: How exactly are you a fan? In what way do you resemble a means of keeping oneself cool?
> DOCTOR: No, it means fanatic, devoted to. Mind you, I've got to say, that American bit in Martin Chuzzlewit, what's that about? Was that just padding or what? I mean, it's rubbish, that bit.
> DICKENS: I thought you said you were my fan.
> DOCTOR: Ah, well, if you can't take criticism.

"The Shakespeare Code" shows the Doctor as a literature fan, gushing as Shakespeare comes onstage:

> DOCTOR: Genius. He's a genius. The genius. The most human human there's ever been. Now we're going to hear him speak. Always he chooses the best words. New, beautiful, brilliant words.
> SHAKESPEARE: Ah, shut your big fat mouths!
> DOCTOR: Oh, well.
> MARTHA: You should never meet your heroes. ("The Shakespeare Code")

Shakespeare in turn parodies badgered celebrities, moaning, "No, no, no. Who let you in? No autographs. No, you can't have yourself sketched with me. And please don't ask where I get my ideas from. Thanks for the interest" ("The Shakespeare Code"). As the Doctor adventures beside the great writers of all time, he fulfills the ultimate fannish dream.

The most amusing of these moments comes when the Tenth Doctor's *mistaken* for a fan…of himself. In the minisode "Time Crash" the Fifth Doctor is annoyed, believing his counterpart to be a fan who has broken into the TARDIS, and complains about the fan groups popping up everywhere. In turn, the Tenth Doctor gushes like a fan (which he actually is) at seeing the Fifth. He notes, "You were *my* Doctor," something often heard from the mobs at conventions. As viewers watch, they're not sure if David Tennant is gushing over Peter Davison or the Tenth Doctor is gushing over the Fifth, or both at once.

The Doctor himself is notably not a fighter or playground bully, but rather a more nerdy intellectual and problem-solver. As such, he echoes his fans in almost every way conceivable. "And that has an enduring appeal: the idea that brute force can be vanquished by intelligence and ingenuity, that a protagonist can triumph despite overwhelming odds. This is how we'd like to believe the world works, even if the evidence from real life suggests that it's not quite true" (Cawley, "Alwyn Turner on Terry Nation"). Laura Mead writes in her teasingly titled essay, "David Tennant's Bum":

> I'd go so far as to argue that the advent of the Doctor as a new kind of sex symbol, the intelligent, pacifist hero, has led to a whole Christmas hamper of other similar characters speckled throughout popular culture, such as Benedict Cumberbatch's Sherlock Holmes. The watershed moment of the "Perfect Ten" Doctor has enabled fans to reappraise the hidden gems of genre television and the other rough diamonds including kindred roles such as Hugh Laurie's House and Nathan Fillion's Malcolm Reynolds. Even the more traditionally swashbuckling roles of Captains Jack Sparrow and the new Kirk now come complete with side orders of emotional angst and ennui. The alpha male, in all

his bullet-spraying glory, is now frequently just a thin veneer
over the more cerebral kind of hero women have grown to
demand. (Kindle Locations 2943-2948).

In addition, the Doctor's entire life is performance – he
keeps his name secret and is forever an outsider. Everywhere he
goes on earth, he plays at being human. He also enjoys fannish
activities like singing (Eighth Doctor), acting (Fourth Doctor),
and playing the spoons (Seventh Doctor) as well as costuming
(all of them). The Doctor is seen drawing beautiful *Doctor Who*
sketches in "Human Nature" and Amy does likewise in "The
Wedding of River Song"…just like their fans do. In several
novels and short stories, he writes science fiction. The Tenth
and Eleventh Doctors in particular are fun and goofy, insisting
on wearing custard mustaches or hiding behind fake personas.
"It is the Doctor's very showmanship that has given the recently
revised series the revered place in the pantheon of science
fiction it enjoys" (Schuster and Powers 7). A few episodes
emphasize the Eleventh Doctor's constant performance as he
tries to fit in, not by being one of the locals but by acting.

> DOCTOR: Now all I've got to do is pass as an ordinary
> human being. Simple. What could possibly go wrong?
> AMY [OC]: Have you seen you?
> DOCTOR: So you're just going to be snide. No helpful
> hints?
> AMY: Hmm. Well, here's one. Bow tie, get rid.
> DOCTOR: Bow ties are cool. Come on, Amy, I'm a normal
> bloke. Tell me what normal blokes do.
> AMY [OC]: They watch telly, they play football. They go
> down the pub.
> DOCTOR: I could do those things. I don't, but I could. ("The
> Lodger")

He air kisses the football players and is oblivious when he's
intruding on Craig's date. When he substitutes at Craig's office
job, adding that he was curious as he's "Never worked in an
office. Never worked in anywhere," he's like a child playing at
work.

On most planets he tries to fit in by assuming an identity

with his psychic paper. "Hello, I'm Captain Troy Handsome of International Rescue. Please state the nature of your emergency," he tells an alien autopilot ("The Lodger"). He's Sir Doctor of TARDIS to Shakespeare and Queen Victoria. In "A Christmas Carol," the paper goes blank when he tells too big a lie – that he's a mature and responsible adult. Shakespeare also emphasizes the Doctor's life as an act.

> SHAKESPEARE: I'll get my answers tomorrow, Doctor, and I'll discover more about you and why this constant performance of yours.
> DOCTOR: All the world's a stage.
> (a quote from *As You Like It,* describing life as a play)
> SHAKESPEARE: Hmm. I might use that. Goodnight, Doctor.
> DOCTOR: Nighty night, Shakespeare. ("The Shakespeare Code")

Companions as Fans

In "Meanwhile in the TARDIS," the short follow-up to Amy's seduction attempt in "Flesh and Stone," the Doctor explains why he has companions:

> DOCTOR: I'm 907. After a while, you just can't see it.
> AMY: See what?!
> DOCTOR: Everything – I look at a star, there's just a big ball of burning gas, and I know how it began and I know how it ends...and I was probably there both times. After a while, everything is just stuff. That's the problem; you make all of space and time your back yard, and what do you have? A back yard. But you; you can see it. And when you see it, I see it.

This emphasis that it's only an adventure if someone is watching it with fresh human eyes reflects on the viewers and emphasizes Amy's role as a viewer stand-in (even one who'd love a fling with the Doctor). Apparently the heart of the Doctor's travels is that human viewers are sharing them.

In "Planet of the Dead," comedian Lee Evans plays

Professor Malcolm Taylor, a UNIT scientist devoted to the Doctor. He's an out-of touch egghead scientist. Upon meeting, he gushes like a fan, thus reflecting the current fandom.

> MAGAMBO: We all want to meet him one day, but we all know what that day will bring.
> DOCTOR: I can hear hear *everything* you're saying!

As the small man on earth who's nonetheless hero of one of the specials, Taylor is an example of a bigger picture. Thus as the stories transfer from the bigger characters to the smaller ones, the text actually subverts itself. It becomes its own parody or fanfiction, an art that often can "pull characters and narrative issues from the margins; they focus on details that are excessive or peripheral to the primary plot but gain significance within the fans' own conceptions of the series" (Jenkins 155). Iona Sharma, author of the essay "All the Way Out to the Stars" explains:

> I once heard someone in fandom comment that all the incidental characters on *Doctor Who* are treated as though they've crossed over from an as-yet-unmade show where they're the star. This is especially true in the year of specials. With no regular companions, the characters who appear in each episode get the bulk of the character development. When Jackson discovers he's not the Doctor after all, but an ordinary man who suffered something terrible, he still steps up - brave and human - when the Doctor needs his help. (Kindle Locations 3469-3472).

Several of the final Tennant specials focus on the importance of ordinary humans – not Donna, the most important woman in the world, but elderly people going about normal lives. Jackson Lake is not the Doctor, but by pretending to be him, he can save the world. In "A Christmas Carol," the Doctor comments: "Nine hundred years of time and space, and I've never met anybody who wasn't important before." When a cross-section of typical Londoners are trapped on a bus on an alien planet, the Doctor asks each of them what matters to them – television, a quiet dinner at home, a girl to ask out. "Chops and gravy," he says, "that's special." He assures them all he'll get them home to continue their lives. In turn, the ordinary people react with heroism:

> Take Nathan and Barclay, the guys on the bus who don't panic when thrown through a wormhole to another planet, and instead ask what they can do to help. Take Malcolm, the socially inept scientist, who flounders and panics and somewhat ridiculously names units of measurement after himself, but who also stands up to UNIT rather than let the passengers on the bus be sacrificed. And there's Angela, who begins the episode crying into her hands, but ends up ready to learn how to drive a bus through space and time. The Doctor, even this sadder, angrier Doctor, understands the potential in people. (Sharma, Kindle Locations 3479-3485).

"The End of Time," more than any other, focuses on the strength of ordinary man. The true hero of this episode is not the Doctor, but Donna's hopeful grandfather Wilfred Mott (Bernard Cribbins). He finds the Doctor by using a network of elderly friends no one else even notices. He also mentors the Doctor, giving him the weapon he'll need to stop the Time Lords and demands he fight to protect earth and himself. In turn, the Doctor sacrifices himself for the elderly human man who's one of the Doctor's biggest fans – for his viewers, especially those who have been there since the beginning. The Tenth Doctor accepts that he is the kind of person who would sacrifice himself for a single human – thus Wilf reminds him who he truly is, as Rose does for the Ninth.

"Blink" is a terribly fannish episode. Not only was it created from Steven Moffat's short story, but it's about fans. The world is saved through the Doctor's "Easter egg" on Sally's seventeen DVDs. Sally's conspiracy nut friend Larry defines it as "Like a DVD extra, yeah? You know how on DVDs they put extras on, documentaries and stuff? Well, sometimes they put on hidden ones, and they call them Easter eggs. You have to go looking for them. Follow a bunch of clues on the menu screen." Larry Nightingale is the ultimate overzealous fan, debating what the

Easter egg means for years and posting a transcript on the net. He believes a "look to your left" comment is political in nature rather than literal, and put another meaningless quote on a t-shirt. His sister describes him as "useless," and he's shocked when she sends a message that she loves him. He's the slobby fan most often seen combing the DVD extras over and over on *Doctor Who* and other popular programs.

Sally and Larry are saved when the TARDIS actually plays a DVD for them – apparently DVDs save lives as well. "Blink," with its unusual minimal appearance by the series regulars, shows a "fan figure" saving the day; as Sue Short notes: "In acquiring the information needed to defeat the menace, as well as saving the Doctor at some point in the future, Sally fulfills a popular fan fantasy" (178). As such, she's a stand-in for the viewers. Likewise, fans watching this episode see the Doctor warning them about the gothic angels found all over the world, as they watch screens within screens, DVDs of DVDs and video of fans. Along with being one of the scariest and impactful episodes, it's also the most fannish.

"Blink" finishes off its homage to the fans with an actual DVD Easter Egg – under Scene Selection, the scene "Keep Looking" has a hidden moment. If one pushes the up button on the remote, the word "Blink" (of course) will highlight. By pressing enter, the Doctor's Easter Egg will play as an Easter Egg, for more self-referential fun. One can even get the script page and speak back.

The most fannish episode is "Love and Monsters," the tale of a *Doctor Who* fan club and its members being absorbed by aliens. The narrator, Elton, is an ordinary young man swept away by his obsession for the Doctor. As he begins, he deconstructs his own performance:

> ELTON [filming a video diary]: I just put that bit at the beginning because it's a brilliant opening, but this is the story of me, and my encounters with alien lifeforms. But be warned, because it is going to get scary. I need a remote control zoom. I'm having to do that with the lean. The scary.

> But look, don't worry, 'because it's not just me sitting here
> talking. Oh, no.

He's an ordinary Londoner, attacked by Slitheen, Autons, and Sycorax, determined to sort out these encounters. Like *Who* fans, he rushes onto the web to discuss what's happening on the show…despite the fact that he's inside it. "So, great big spaceship hanging over London. Imagine the theories. The internet went into meltdown. But I kept on digging. Something was going on. Oh, yes. And then one day, on some obscure little blog by someone called Ursula Blake, it was like a chance in a million."

They organize and find a meeting place, name themselves, start cooking together, form a band. In short, they're having fun together and becoming a social group. Mr. Skinner, the academic, begins writing a book and reading it aloud. Skinner analyzes their fandom with a scholarly approach, calling the Doctor a "collection of archetypes." Another friend presents slideshows of his activities. There's an artist and a blogger and a video maker…in short, a spectrum of fandom.

Henry Jenkins describes organized fandom as "an institution of theory and criticism, a semistructured space where competing interpretations and evaluations of common texts are proposed, debated, and negotiated and where readers speculate about the nature of the mass media and their own relationship to it" (86). As the self-named fans of LINDA analyze, debate, and discuss, they're a fan group like the many *Who* groups watching the show together.

Unfortunately, their group is taken over by (apparently) the pushy fan who tells them they're enjoying fandom "wrong," the one who must ruin everyone's good time. "You've forgotten your purpose in life. You, with your band and your cakes and your blubbing and all the while he still exists. The Doctor," Victor grumbles. He gives out homework assignments and turns their fun space into a classroom. Metaphorically he's devouring the group, and as so often happens, his monstrousness turns literal as he's an alien cannibal. The Absorbaloff tries to absorb everyone, an angry fan who wishes to own all of fandom. Only the Doctor, champion of the little people, even his own obsessive fans, manages to save the day.

The Doctor as Costumer

"As traditional as his clothing often is, there is usually something "off" about it to stress the Doctor's individuality, such as the tenth Doctor's insistence on wearing a shirt and tie, a pinstriped suit, and... red sneakers?" (DiPaolo 965-966). Each Doctor was known for his particular outfit, beginning with the first: "Hartnell's frock coat and Dickensian attitude make him seem a refugee from the world of Conan Doyle, gaslight, hansom cabs, imperial adventure and Jack the Ripper" (Newman 16). It also hints at H.G. Wells and a Steampunk sensibility. "Subsequent Doctors have retained period fashion sense: shabby-genteel Troughton, dashing Pertwee (in color, adding a scarlet lining to his ulster as Hammer's Dracula did to his cloak), Edwardian cricketeer Davison, Wild Bill Hickock-costumed McGann" (Newman 16). Tom Baker is known for his cascading scarf and odd hat. His coat would subtly change color depending on the genre of the particular serial--yellow-brown for adventure, red for action, and grey for horror or mystery. "The 'off'ness of the Doctor's clothing not only contributes to the 'alien'ness of the character but also makes a determination about the Doctor's economic class and sexual orientation difficult to pin down" (DiPaolo 965-966). However, by the time of the Fifth through Seventh Doctors, each man had only one outfit, as if dressing in his daily uniform:

- Most Doctors wear costumes: the First Doctor has a plumed French hat and matching uniform in "Reign of Terror" and a cowboy hat in "The Gunfighters."
- The Second Doctor wears a stovepipe, bobble hat, and headscarf in various episodes.
- The Third Doctor stood out in the flamboyant and overly-colorful seventies by dressing even more

outrageously – he was known for velvet smoking jackets, ruffled poet shirts, a black silk cravat, and even a sweeping cape, like a mediaeval troubadour racing through England in his bright yellow car, Bessie. His old fashioned dress offered an aristocratic look and also linked him to John Steed of the terribly popular *The Avengers*, famous for the then-out-of-date bowler hat.

• In the Fourth Doctor's first episode, he tries a full Viking warrior's costume as his "look," then appears in a king's costume and an Italian clown, complete with garish colors and tinsel. His fourth attempt is his Fourth Doctor "look" with brown hat and lengthy scarf, emphasizing this outfit is a costume as well. While this last remains, the Fourth Doctor neglects his attire: waistcoats are left sloppily unbuttoned, or his fedora is crammed into his pocket. Several critics compare him to Harpo Marx, the curly-haired comic tramp (Britton 46).

• The Fifth Doctor wears a cricket outfit with a stalk of celery in his lapel, something only explained in his final appearance.

• "Christopher Eccleston wore a crew cut and a black leather jacket and played the Doctor as the personification of John Lennon's iconic Working-Class Hero in the first season of Davies' revival" (DiPaolo 965-966). He may be the least colorful dresser of them all, fitting as he traumatized and angry from the war.

• The Tenth Doctor has a blazing bright blue suit and running shoes (or occasionally, a tux and running shoes). Tennant apparently "begged producers to base his style on that of British celebrity chef Jaime Oliver" (Goodall 78). He also requested the comfortable trainers.

• The Eleventh dresses as a nutty professor with tweed and bowtie, sporting "a Professor-from-*Gilligan's Island* allure" (Nussbaum 127). His old-fashioned wardrobe (and hopeless insistence that it's cool) contrasted with his youthful face gives him a strange, otherworldy

67

quality. Matt Smith and Patrick Troughton (the Second Doctor) are both aping the "conventional 'boffin' of screen science fiction, with his untidy hair, bow tie, and baggy, unflattering attire" (Britton 43).

Smith acts, dances, and performs while "waving" to his friends out of history books. In one old film, Smith is wearing a colossal turban. In "A Christmas Carol," he wears a Santa hat. Eleven adds other garish examples of cosplay, like a fez and Stetson. Despite his claims, the other characters believe neither is cool.

> The first four Doctors have a style but not a specific costume: when in Tibet, Troughton wore a shaggy fur coat, for instance; and even Pertwee has a wardrobe of different frilly shirts, velvet jackets, and caped ulsters. From the middle of Tom Baker's tenure, each Doctor unvaryingly sports their own distinctive, question-mark-pocked uniform as if dressing up as themselves. It's a comic-book convention, unsustainable in live-action where audiences wonder if the hero is indeed wearing the same never-cleaned, never-worn-out clothes for years on end. (Newman 97)

The Seventh Doctor transforms his coat from white to dark brown, just as his stories get darker and edgier. However, his question-mark pattered vest and question-mark cane make him seem more circus performer than conventional gentleman. "McCoy's outfit seemed like a childish conflation of past Doctors' dress: The Fifth's panama hat, the Second's check trousers, the First's spectator shoes, and so on" (Britton 50).

The Eighth Doctor arrives at Halloween, appropriately resuscitating in a morgue while the attendant is watching *Frankenstein*. The Eighth Doctor's outfit is full Victorian; he steals it from an actual Wild Bill Hickok costume, and discards the gunbelt and hat. (Thus the Third, Eighth, and Eleventh Doctors all steal their outfits from hospital lockers.) On the Eighth Doctor's audio and comic adventures, he keeps the same outfit, though it grows shabbier, and he finally replaces it with a similar cut but simpler materials. Eight of the eleven Doctors are seen deliberately choosing costumes in their first adventure. "They gave quite literally dressed the part within the narrative" (Britton 53). This reminds viewers that this new Doctor is a role, as the previous one was as well.

In *New Who,* the Doctors revert to a style rather than a uniform – the Tenth Doctor has two favorite suits and multiple colors of trainers, along with his sometimes-optional favorite coat. The Eleventh Doctor has different bow ties, and Rory is horrified to discover he has two tweed jackets, both equally fashion mistakes.

- The Eleventh Doctor costumes with accessories – bow ties, a fez, a Stetson, along with his unfortunate insistence that all these things are cool…Amy and River pause in saving the world long enough to use the fez for target practice. He wears a pirate hat in "The Curse of the Black Spot."
- The Doctor's bowtie in his eleventh incarnation will be red if the episode takes place in the future, and blue if it's in the past. Also, his coat, is a much darker brown after the gloomy events of "The Angels Take Manhattan."
- In "The Bells of Saint John" the Doctor plays many uncharacteristic roles: he's a hermit monk in the 12th century, a computer help line, a James-Bond style hero in contemporary London with an antigrav motorcycle, and finally one of the spoonhead devices.
- In the Children in Need special, "The Doctor's Clothes," the Doctor strips and offers his clothes up for charity auction. He describes a jacket "made of infinity tweed" and "hyper trousers," the sort of additions many fans make at cons when they add color to their backstories.
- The real Matt Smith himself has been known to costume, designing one in particular: Matt was the one to create the bowtie and suspenders look, against

Moffat's objections, as he thought it was too ridiculous. As soon as Matt was in his chosen outfit, though, he rethought matters and his Doctor's entire wardrobe was changed about half a day before the deadline. "I was always very keen that the element of the professor would come out," says Smith (Masters). Describing future changes in his costume, he noted: "I want a coat - practically - because I get cold. And I'd quite like a hat..." (Masters). His wish for several unusual hats was granted throughout the series.

🎀 In an attempt to explore Comic-Con while incognito, Smith tried cosplaying in a Bart Simpson mask. He enjoys fandom extremely, noting, "Look, it's a slough and it's hard, but ultimately you're making *Doctor Who*, so who cares?! Yeah, I'll sleep more, but no one will be screaming when I walk into a room full of people, dressed in fezzes. I'll miss all the cool stuff that comes with it." (Radish, "Matt Smith")

Companions' Costumes

The Doctor and his companions have issues as they travel to all sorts of planets, and only occasionally dress for the occasion. Now and then they dress for Victorian times, from the Eleventh Doctor's top hat or bowler to the Fourth Doctor's Sherlock Holmes getup. Most often, especially in modern or future settings, the Doctors wear their standard outfit and the locals accept it without pause (of course, some ensembles like the Sixth Doctor's horrid coat of primary colors or the Fifth Doctor's cricket gear don't fit in anywhere – that's part of the joke). The companions' standard dress reflects their eras and jobs, from Tegan's stewardess uniform to Susan's youthful teen dresses in the sixties. Jeans and various leather jackets are popular among Tennant's companions, soon replaced by Amy's famed miniskirts.

🎀 In "The Unquiet Dead," the Doctor tells Rose to change into a more Victorian outfit or "You'll start a riot, Barbarella!" The Doctor by contrast just puts on a different sweater and Dickens assumes he's a "navy."

◆ In "The Empty Child," Rose wears jeans and a Union Jack T-shirt (Jack comments the fabric is too modern) while the Doctor is in his usual leather jacket – an embarrassing clash as it mimics one worn by German U-Boat captains.

◆ Amy Pond wears a mini-skirt nearly everywhere and characters like Van Gogh and Churchill don't complain...just flirt.

> MALOKEH: The female seems more resistant to the cold than the male.
> AMY: I dressed for Rio! ("Cold Blood")

◆ In "Tooth and Claw," Rose wears a denim minidress to visit 1979. When they end up in 1879, the soldiers call her a "wee naked child" and Queen Victoria orders her into a more appropriate outfit.

◆ Clara Oswin Oswald appears as starliner entertainment officer, Victorian barmaid, proper governess, and modern woman. The governess appears to be a disguise of her actual lower-class self, and the entertainment officer is a self-delusion and disguise of a sort, as she's been transformed into a Dalek.

◆ River Song enjoys all sorts of outfits, masquerading as Cleopatra or dressing as a femme fatale with high heels and sunglasses, to say nothing of the hallucinogenic lipstick.

> RIVER: [after taking down five Nazi police] Thanks, boys! Call me!
> AMY: What are you doing?!
> RIVER: New body, new rules... I'm going shopping! ("Let's Kill Hitler")

She tries on a Nazi hat and coat and exclaims she loves jodhpurs. In an extra scene from *The Brilliant Book 2012*, young Mels is described as "excellent in drama, especially at pretending to be someone else" on her report card (103).

- Amy spends much of her first episode in her police uniform (adding that it was that or a naughty nurse). An elderly woman in town is puzzled over her many apparent jobs. However, Amy does use her police uniform to bully her way into the necessary hospital wing, using it for more than her kissogram connections.
- In the spinoff novel *The Many Hands*, Martha journeys to 18th century Edinburgh. When a soldier criticizes her for wearing "pantaloons," she sarcastically asks if it's against the law. In fact, it is.
- Visiting Pompeii, Donna asks whether her jeans will be conspicuous. The Doctor retorts, "Nah, ancient Rome? It's like Soho. Anything goes." Nonetheless, Donna tries out a stola and gown while visting. Ironically, they're revealed as jarringly foreign whenever the Doctor uses Latin expressions – each sounds like Celtic to the locals.
- Famously in "The Talons of Weng-Chiang," the Doctor dresses as Sherlock Holmes (complete with deerstalker) to solve a Victorian mystery. Leela, typically found in a leather bikini, dons a lovely Victorian gown. She tears her first one fighting and must order a (prettier) replacement. Despite this, Leela continues to act like a barbarian in her eating habits as she dives into a buffet by gnawing on a leg of lamb without plate, carving knife, or utensils. Her bemused yet polite host follows suit.
- The action-powered eighties girl Ace is similarly told to put on a Victorian gown in her adventure of "Ghost Light." Amusingly, she indeed puts on Victorian garb – a man's suit.
- Similarly, in medieval times, Sarah Jane dresses like Robin Hood, not a fainting damsel.
- Sarah Jane wears a previous companion's white gown in the Fourth Doctor adventure *Pyramids of Mars*.

- At the end of "The Seeds of Doom," the TARDIS journeys to the wrong place and Sarah Jane Smith walks into Antarctica in a swimsuit.
- In *The Sarah Jane Adventures* story "The Temptation of Sarah Jane Smith," teenage Rani Chandra time travels back to 1951. She assumes she's getting strange looks because she's Indian, but it's her clothes that shock everyone. By contrast, Sarah Jane deliberately dresses for the time, noting that "The 50s came back in the 70s."

Who's Behind *Who*

Creator References

🎀 Gareth Roberts, writer of "The Shakespeare Code," had a deep interest in Shakespeare, and had included him in his 2005 Ninth Doctor comic strip "A Groatsworth of Wit" in *Doctor Who Magazine*.

🎀 Writer Mark Gatiss re-uses a few ideas from his audio adventure *Phantasmagoria*. On "The Unquiet Dead," Charles Dickens shouts "What phantasmagoria is this?!" Gatiss wrote novels such as *Nightshade* and *St Anthony's Fire* for Virgin Publishing's *Doctor Who*: The New Adventures series in 1992. He even played the Master in the Doctor Who Unbound play *Sympathy for the Devil*, then appeared as the Doctor on a sketch for BBC2's Doctor Who Night in 1999. He also filmed the Mockumentary Global Conspiracy, based on the Third Doctor serial "The Green Death."

🎀 "Rise of the Cybermen"/"The Age of Steel" mentioned "Paula Moore," creator of "Attack of the Cybermen."

🎀 Steven Moffat saluted outgoing executive producers Beth Willis and Piers Wenger in "The Doctor, the Widow, and the Wardrobe" by naming Ven-Garr and Billis after them.

🎀 In "Human Nature," the human Doctor says his parents' names were Sydney and Verity; two of the show's original creators were Sydney Newman and Verity Lambert. Joan Redfern's granddaughter, seen in "The End of Time," is named Verity Newman (and they're played by the same actress).

➤ In the original series episode "The Robots of Death," "Grimwade's Syndrome," a fear of robots, is named for director Peter Grimwade, who hated robot stories. The character Poul is presumably after science fiction writer Poul Anderson. Uvanov is a reference to Isaac Asimov, and Taren Capel to Karel Capek, inventor of the word "robot."

Davies's Shared References

> Of course, Davies has always mixed entertainment with activism, most notably in his miniseries The Second Coming (2003), a political fantasy in which he posited what would happen if a new Messiah would be born into modern-day England. By the end of the story, the Messiah's girlfriend convinces him that God, and all organized religion, holds humanity back by fostering a global culture of ignorance and violence. In response, the savior obliges her, and humanity, by killing himself. Davies is also famous for writing the series Bob and Rose, about a gay man who falls in love with a woman. In the series, the couple encounters prejudice from members of both the gay and the straight communities. As Davies explained in a 2001 article he wrote for The Observer, he intended to surround Bob and Rose with an array of "cardboard" villains but fleshed out the characterizations of their enemies by revealing that everyone has something to hide, and everyone has some "coming out" to do ("A Rose by Any Other Name"). (DiPaolo 972)

Davies wrote many series before *Doctor Who*, and most contain nods to one another. *The Second Coming* featured Christopher Eccleston and his *Casanova* starred David Tennant (both led to his offering them the role of the Doctor). His stories are provocative, with unusual premises, and terribly funny quick moments. In "The New Man: The Regeneration of Doctor Who," Dave Hoskin writes, "Davies' comedy style, for example, has always tended to accentuate the outrageous. *Queer as Folk* makes us laugh because of the protagonists' gleeful transgression of social norms, while *Mine All Mine* revolves around the fundamentally ridiculous idea of a man inheriting the city of Swansea" (132). *Mine All Mine* (2004) was set in Davies' home town of Swansea, and attempted to share Welsh family life with a mass audience. *Torchwood* takes place in Cardiff as do *Who* episodes "The Unquiet Dead" and "Boom Town," carrying the audience back to Davies' home country.

Queer as Folk may be Davies' most famous project before *Doctor Who,* as he attempted to make, as he put it, "The definitive gay series. Gay men and lesbians, older men, mothers, fag-hags, closets and camp, homophobia and HIV...a crippling responsibility. So I made the best decision of all." He chose to write exactly what he wanted – a story of hijinks and relationships as his characters struggle with family, identity, and relationships. He calls it "A good story, with a good laugh, and the odd bit of heartbreak along the way" (Davies, "Transmission").

Century Falls was written about, as Davies puts it, "That dark, sinister English village. Which the *League of Gentlemen* has now ruined forever! I like taking those old, classic ideas, and reinventing them - not to spoil them, but to make them relevant to each new generation" ("Interview: Writer Russell T Davies: Century Falls"). It features fat children, gawky, unlikeable children – outcasts seeking acceptance, like the characters of *Queer as Folk, Torchwood,* or *The Sarah Jane Adventures.* Davies describes the children as "One nice, one nasty, one stuck in the middle. Again, it's archetypal. You could use the same description for the *Queer as Folk* trio" ("Interview: Writer Russell T Davies: Century Falls").

Davies has several children's series that echo *Doctor Who,* in which a lead character and several "companions" investigate unusual activities. All are written in two-part adventures, echoing the Doctor's multi-part style. *The Sarah Jane Adventures* is the most obvious of these, with Sarah Jane's adopted semi-alien children Luke and Sky solving alien-related mysteries along with the neighbor children Maria, Clyde, and Rani. However, similar series existed before and after.

Davies' first series, *Dark Season,* is similar. It follows third year secondary school girl Marcie and her two fifth year friends Tom and Reet (the latter was played by Kate Winslet in her first major professional acting role). "I was working as a producer in Children's BBC, and was dying to write the sort of shows I'd enjoyed as a kid," he explains ("Interview - writer Russell T Davies"). In an homage to Fourth Doctor's companion Leela, Davies had Reet use a yo-yo to test gravity. He adds, "I just wanted to get rid of all the padding, and make Marcie very aware that she was in a sci-fi drama. So she had an omniscience, which then made her Doctor-ish" ("Interview – writer Russell T Davies: Dark Season").

Davies trapped Rose Tyler behind a door that refused to open in "The End of the World" – just as he had done with Reet in episode six of *Dark Season*. When challenged by their rescuers not to go anywhere, both characters offered the same response: "Where am I gonna go, Ipswich?" *Dark Season* was a school show, echoing "School Reunion," which soon became one (though originally set on an army base). "The Next Doctor," recasts elements of the *Dark Season* Behemoth as the CyberKing, with the lead female villains in both trying to take over the world this way and thus being trapped inside the monster. Davies adds, describing this last:

> The first gay character I ever wrote was a Devil-worshipping Nazi lesbian in a Children's BBC thriller, Dark Season. She was too busy taking over the world to do anything particularly lesbian, though she did keep a Teutonic Valkyrie by her side at all times. Like you do. (Davies, "Transmission")

After *The Sarah Jane Adventures,* Davies created his next children's series. *Wizards vs Aliens* is basically a replacement for *The Sarah Jane Adventures.* Other writers working on the show include Gareth Roberts, Joseph Lidster and Clayton Hickman. Brian Miller, Elisabeth Sladen's husband, appeared in the first story. The second series also uses "The Thirteenth Floor," a script written for the fifth series of *The Sarah Jane Adventures.*

In one of the most blatant ties between his series, Davies

mentions that reusing names (including Tyler, Smith, Harper, Harkness and Jones) helps him get an instant grip of the character (Pryor). Thus, Martha and her family share the last name "Jones" with many other Russell T Davies characters:

- Harriet Jones in *Doctor Who*
- Ianto Jones and Eugene Jones in *Torchwood*
- Yanto Jones in *Mine All Mine*
- Stuart Allen Jones in *Queer as Folk*

Other *Queer as Folk* characters include main character Vince Tyler, a supermarket manager (echoing shopgirl Rose Tyler) and familiar first names Donna Clark and Rosalie Cotter. Characters with the surname Tyler also appear in *Revelations, Damaged Goods*, and *The Second Coming*.

- *The Grand,* Davies' British costume drama series set in a hotel in Manchester in the 1920s, offers more similar names: The Bannerman family runs the hotel, with chambermaid Monica Jones and footman/bartender Clive. Davies notes, "Clive was a working-class lad struggling to express his sexuality in a time when the proper adjectives and nouns barely even existed. And by focusing on Clive's sexuality instead of subplotting it, I wrote better" (Davies, "Transmission"). Guests included Esme Harkness, an allegedly former prostitute.
- *Century Falls* also has a character named Esme Harkness.
- *Torchwood* echoes Davies' earlier works: Gwen is heart, faith, and normalcy on the show as she drags her inept boyfriend about, much like Rose. Captain Jack comes across as a hybrid of the Doctor and Stuart from *Queer as Folk*, while Ianto becomes progressively more like Vince.
- Tricia Delaney is mentioned in *Doctor Who* and Philip Delaney appeared in *Queer as Folk*.
- Gareth David-Lloyd plays Ianto Jones in *Torchwood*, after playing *Yanto* Jones in Davies' *Mine All Mine*.
- Russell T Davies was planning to make a show about science fiction criminal investigators. He had planned to name it Excalibur, until it evolved into the *Doctor*

79

Who spin-off *Torchwood*. In the episode "Kiss Kiss Bang Bang" John Hart suggests Excalibur as a better name.

- John Hart is playing "Starship Trooper" when Jack comes to confront him at the end of series two. The same song is used for a funeral in *Queer as Folk*.
- In Davies' *The Second Coming*, Christopher Eccleston plays the son of God. The Doctor of course has several invincible and godlike moments.
- Davies is also known for the show *Bob & Rose*, about unrequited love. "Like Vince (Craig Kelly) in *Queer as Folk*, Holly (Jessica Hynes) in *Bob & Rose* or even Casanova, the Doctor's companions quietly pined for someone they couldn't have" (Hoskin 133).
- In "Smith and Jones," Davies chose to name its administrator after Mr Stoker from his earlier show *Children's Ward*. The design team assumed this was a reference to *Dracula*'s author Bram Stoker, and stamped "B Stoker" on the office door.
- In "The Stolen Earth," Harriet Jones transfers the subwave network to Captain Jack. A map of Swansea (Davies' hometown) pops up instead of Cardiff.

Damaged Goods, Davies' Virgin New Adventures novel (featuring the Seventh Doctor) reflects some of his other works. There's a Tyler family once again – Tylers also appear in *Revelations, Queer as Folk, and The Second Coming*. In the novel, Davies mentions his television works, referencing *Why Don't You* and *Dark Season*'s Marcie. Davies' novel as well as *The Second Coming* features a character's meal being laced with poison. A Time Lord's amazing sense of smell appears in the novel, and then in the Eccleston era. The novel's Doctor is horrified by "family time," just as the Ninth Doctor is. He notes: "I'd find it easier to gain access to the court of Rassilon himself, than to step over Winnie Tyler's front door" (56). "The End of Time" as well as the novel feature hiding a picosecond ahead in time. A final intriguing quote from the novel reminds readers of "The Empty Child": "The Voice was cruel, mimicking the cry she longed to hear. Mu mmy Mu mmy Mu mmy" (122). A copy of the novel appeared in *Who* fan Vince's bedroom on *Queer as Folk.*

Moffat's Shared References

> Moffat, on the other hand, is a specialist in farce. Just as his previous shows Chalk and Coupling use misunderstandings to create intricate comedy situations, his monsters are motivated by similar lacunae. Thus the grotesque Empty Child is the creation of alien medical technology that doesn't understand human physiology, and as in most farce, the story's resolution occurs when the characters allow their secrets into the open. (Hoskin 132)

The Moffat episodes stand out on *Doctor Who:* "The Empty Child"/"The Doctor Dances," "The Girl in the Fireplace," "Blink," "Silence in the Library"/"Forest of the Dead." All are particular fan favorites, defined by creepy, silent monsters but also moments of humor and heart. Fans were delighted when he was announced as showrunner. "When Davies was asked to identify the story Moffat kept returning to over and over again, his answer was similarly perceptive: parenthood. It's there in *Press Gang, Jekyll, Coupling,* and the four stories Moffat wrote for Davies, all of them bar one featuring children in danger," Hoskin notes (133).

To start his television career, Moffat wrote the school show *Chalk* and school newspaper show *Press Gang* based on his own teaching experiences. In fact, Big Finish Productions, which produces many *Doctor Who* audio dramas, among others, was named after *Press Gang*'s second series finale. Moffat's next idea was about "a sitcom writer whose wife leaves him," and his *Joking Apart* lasted two years ("Fool if You Think It's Over"). Sadly, the show lasted longer than his marriage. The main character was Mark Taylor – Steve Taylor was the hero of his following series.

Moffat's *Coupling* was about his relationship with his second wife, TV producer Sue Vertue. It became known as the British version of *Friends* – the show of five twenty-something friends struggling through the British dating scene. It was concerned with relationships and used clever visual gags to make its playful entendres. Meanwhile, Oliver Morris, the boyfriend of the final year, is an avid fan with many *Doctor Who* decorations in his science fiction shop.

Coupling had several very popular nonlinear stories, with scenes shown from a non-English speaker's point of view or with a single nine and a half minute time segment recast through multiple people's lives. Likewise, the first six episodes of *Joking Apart* were mostly built non-sequentially, with the characters' love story and later divorce story combined through flashbacks. Moffat describes his non-linear technique as a "romantic comedy, but a romantic comedy backwards because it ends with the couple unhappy" ("Fool if You Think It's Over"). *Press Gang* also plays with out-of-sequence adventures, especially in the episode "Monday-Tuesday." The frequent device of showing a scene from two points of view, entirely changing the meaning of what occurs finds its echo in the constantly-rewritten history of the Eleventh Doctor's life with Amy, River, and Clara in turn.

The miniseries *Jekyll* uses Moffat's skill with shock and horror to surprise the audience several times over. It's not precisely a retelling or a modernization of Stevenson's short story, but contains elements of both. Family relationships, from siblings to parents and spouses, are at the center of this tale, as an ordinary man must face the dark savage inside himself and find a way to negotiate a peace, even as he explores the secrets of the past.

Moffat's *Sherlock,* basically a modern rewrite of the original stories, contains even more references to the original source than his *New Who* does to *Old Who* – and that's saying something! Every moment is clever and witty, while the young yet self-absorbed and asexual Holmes has many echoes with the Doctor himself. And of course both rely on their companions to provide normalcy to balance their extraordinary gifts. Moffat continues to write *Sherlock* and *Who* at once, earning fans' devotion for both series.

- Moffat had first used the line "Life is just nature's way of keeping meat fresh" in the second series of his 1990s sitcom *Joking Apart,* then uses it again in "The Doctor Dances" The Chula ships of that episode are named after Chula a fusion restaurant in Hammersmith, London where the writers celebrated and discussed their briefs on the scripts they were to write for the year after being commissioned by Russell T Davies ("The Doctor Dances" commentary).
- "Forest of the Dead" names Donna's "children" Josh and Ella. Josh is Steven Moffat's son's name, and Ella is his friend.
- In "Let's Kill Hitler," the scene where the Doctor explains he anticipated Melody's plans is filmed similarly to *Sherlock.* The whole sequence where the Doctor and Melody one-up each other's attempts to assassinate or stop the other echoes the television parody *Doctor Who: The Curse of Fatal Death*, also written by Steven Moffat.
- The line "I've put a lot of work into it" (re: the Earth/universe) in "The Eleventh Hour" comes from *Doctor Who: The Curse of Fatal Death.*
- River's archaeology professor at Luna University is named in the end credits as Professor Candy. This professor and location hail from Moffat's short story "Continuity Errors," as is the "I had yesterday off" joke.
- "Continuity Errors" and the episode "A Christmas Carol" both feature changing someone's mind by changing their pasts to make them nicer.

> DOCTOR: It's just a nightmare, Reinette, don't worry, everyone has nightmares. Even monsters under the bed have nightmares.
> YOUNG REINETTE: What do monsters have nightmares about?
> DOCTOR: Me! ("The Girl in the Fireplace")

This dialogue is repeated from Steven Moffat's first *Doctor Who* story, "Continuity Errors," which in turn is repeated from Paul Cornell's "Love and War."

- When Moffat was assigned "Blink," he based it on the short story he had written for the *Doctor Who Annual 2006*, entitled "What I Did on my Christmas Holidays by Sally Sparrow." He updated his twelve year-old heroine, but kept the cryptic messages the stranded Doctor leaves her behind wallpaper, in photographs, and on a videocassette. Moffat named his story "Sally Sparrow and the Weeping Angels." When its title was changed to "Blink," he memorably added the word in as many places as possible.
- In "The Eleventh Hour" the guy who's surfing porn and seriously needs to get a girlfriend's name is Jeff. Jeff on *Coupling* has a similar constant fetish.
- The Doctor gives many deductions about Kazran's Scroogelike father (presented in the rapid-fire style of Moffat's other hit show of 2010, *Sherlock*).
- Clive Wood, the Roman commander in "The Pandorica Opens," and Lee Ross, the Boatswain in "The Curse of the Black Spot" previously starred in *Press Gang*.
- In "The Snowmen," the Eleventh Doctor spoofs Sherlock Holmes has he clumsily struggles to solve crimes, winking at the show *Sherlock*.

Cameos

- Writer Mark Gatiss appeared briefly in "Victory of the Daleks" and "A Good Man Goes to War" (He's a pilot in the former).
- The Fifth Doctor's real life daughter is the title character in the aptly named "The Doctor's Daughter." Georgia Moffett had also appeared alongside her father in the 2000 Doctor Who audio play *Red Dawn* from Big Finish Productions. She auditioned for the role of Robina Redmond in "The Unicorn and the Wasp" before offered her own episode.

- David Tennant's father Alexander McDonald plays a footman in "The Unicorn and the Wasp," while visiting David on set.
- David Tennant suggested that Fenella Woolgar play Agatha Christie – he'd previously worked with her on *Bright Young Things* and *He Knew He Was Right*.
- Likewise seen in "The Unicorn and the Wasp," Christopher Benjamin (Colonel Curbishley), appeared in the old Who episodes "Inferno" (1970) and "The Talons of Weng-Chiang" (1977).
- Harry the caretaker in *The Sarah Jane Adventures'* "The Mad Woman in the Attic" is played by Elisabeth Sladen's real-life husband, Brian Miller.
- The Eighth Doctor audio "An Earthly Child" features Paul McGann's (The Eighth Doctor's) actual son as the Doctor's great-grandson by Susan.
- In a scene cut from "The Runaway Bride," David Tennant's parents, sister-in-law, and two young nieces were meant to play extras.
- Anne Robinson of *The Weakest Link,* Davina McCall of *Big Brother,* and Trinny Woodall and Susannah Constantine of *What Not To Wear* all leant their vocal talents to the evil robots on "Bad Wolf."
- In "Army of Ghosts" Trisha Goddard plays herself on her own talk show. Barbara Windsor also supplied a fake *EastEnders* scene, in character as Peggy Mitchell.
- "The Sound Of Drums" /"Last Of The Time Lords" hosted celebrities Sharon Osbourne, pop group McFly, and Ann Widdecomb, all endorsing Harold Saxon.
- John Leeson voiced K-9 in "School Reunion." He was the original K-9 twice on *Doctor Who,* and also for *K-9 and Company, The Five Doctors, Shada*, and the Gallifrey audio series from Big Finish.
- Originally, Martha Jones was supposed to appear in the finale of *The Sarah Jane Adventures: Series Two* (she was replaced with the Brigadier thanks to her scheduling conflicts with *Law and Order: UK*) Had this happened,

she would have been the first and only character to appear on all three shows, aside from a few newscasters.

Actor References

Just as the creators like to mention their past shows, reuse actors and bits of dialogue, and otherwise nod to their past creations, they include nods to their top actors and the previous parts they've played, as Tennant rejects a Casanova coat and Hogwarts gown for his pinstripe suit, or Matt Smith shows off soccer skills from before he began acting. These are fun moments for fans, placing their heroes in a larger world of fiction while reminded that this is just another acting job, albeit a dream one for *Who* fans like these.

David Tennant

34-year-old David Tennant replaced 41-year-old Christopher Eccleston, bringing "a legion of female admirers won largely through his two recent acclaimed television roles, in Peter Bowker's *Blackpool,* and Russell T Davies's equally left-field and compelling *Casanova.*" (Merritt, Kindle Locations 626-628). As Laura Mead admiringly notes, "Here was a previously low-profile actor, now being voted as Attitude's man of the year, and ranked Sixteenth Most Sexy Man worldwide by *Cosmopolitan* in 2008" (Kindle Locations 2848-2850).

A longtime *Doctor Who* fan, Tennant appeared in several Big Finish audio dramas, including *Colditz* as Feldwebel Kurtz and *Medicinal Purposes* as Daft Jamie. He also had a small part in in *Scream of the Shalka* and narrated the BBC1 show *Doctor Who: A New Dimension* just before being cast. David Tennant was terribly excited to act alongside Elisabeth Sladen and Peter Davison, whom he grew up watching on the show. His life as a fan is considered to be one of the reasons his Tenth Doctor was truly excellent. He became one of the most popular Doctors of all time.

➤ Malcolm's unit of measurement for four-dimensional phenomena in "Planet of the Dead" is named in honor of Bernard Quatermass – David Tennant and Mark Gatiss starred in the 2005 remake of *The Quatermass Experiment.* Professor Lazarus's monstrous death in the church appears to be another reference to it.

- In "The End of Time," The Doctor is told that "The universe will sing you to your rest," a *Hamlet* altered quote, after David Tennant starred in the live play.
- The Eleventh Doctor mentions he owes the author Casanova a chicken in "The Vampires of Venice." In fact, David Tennant starred in Russell T. Davies's *Casanova* miniseries, and thus became Davies' choice for the Tenth Doctor. Tennant considers wearing the Casanova coat in the "The Christmas Invasion," before choosing the suit and brown overcoat instead.

Matt Smith

Matt Smith gushes, "That's the weird thing with me now, going from someone who didn't really watch *Doctor Who* that much, now that I'm a fan watching loads of it, you can never really…well I can never really switch that off when I meet people like Lis [Elisabeth Sladen]" (Hickman 14).

Apparently, Matt Smith wrote *Doctor Who* fanfic to get in touch with his character. (It involved the Doctor meeting Einstein, amusingly the same theme a classroom of children picked for the adventure they wrote, which won a contest and was in fact televised as "Death Is the Only Answer" by the Children of Oakley Junior School.). Smith adds, "I wrote loads of stories about the Doctor and Einstein in Egypt - that's how the pyramids were created…I had six months, and it was the only way that I could get in contact with the Doctor" (Masters).

- Smith also kissed Rory in an unscripted moment that went on camera, and he invented the catchphrase "Come along, Pond."
- In "The Doctor's Clothes, a minisode, the Eleventh Doctor does a striptease for charity. His comment, "There's more where this came from" may reference his very naked make out session with a very hot man in the

movie, *Christopher and His Kind*. In the minisode he interacts with the audience, suggesting they have a remote that will delete his clothing piece by piece.

- Smith was an Isherwood fan before playing him in *Christopher and His Kind*. Christopher Isherwood is a homosexual writer caught in Nazi Germany; Smith returns there in "Let's Kill Hitler."
- Smith starred with Billie Piper in an episode of *Secret Diary of a Call Girl* and the Sally Lockhart television films *The Ruby in the Smoke* and *The Shadow in the North*.
- In the episode "The Lodger" the Doctor shows off his soccer skills from his pre-acting days.
- Smith previously auditioned for the part of Watson in *Sherlock,* so when the Doctor tries to make deductions as "Sherlock Holmes," he's absolutely rubbish at it. Smith said in interviews, "I think Mark and Steven kind of hate the idea of Doctor Who and Sherlock ever meeting....I'm not averse to it. I'm kind of open" (Weintraub).

Peter Capaldi

Peter Capaldi is another fan-turned-Doctor, who even wrote articles for *Doctor Who* fanzines in the 1970s. A teen Capaldi wrote "loads of letters" to *Doctor Who,* and finally received a package from producer Barry Letts. "It contained set designs and studio floor plans," Capaldi said in an interview. "That was a trigger to my ambition to work in TV" (Collis, "Doctor Who?").

While he won an Oscar for writing and directing *Franz Kafka's It's a Wonderful Life* and played political operative Malcolm Tucker on the BBC's *The Thick of It,* he's known among British speculative fiction fans for his ethereal, complex portrayal of the Angel Islington in Neil Gaiman's *Neverwhere* from the BBC, and his haunting John Frobisher from the *Torchwood* miniseries "Children of Earth." He's had other science fiction and fantasy parts as well. "Capaldi was most recently seen playing, eerily, a WHO doctor (as in World Health

VALERIE ESTELLE FRANKEL

Organization) alongside Brad Pitt in the Wales-set climax of
World War Z. He also has a role in the forthcoming thriller
Maleficent starring Angelina Jolie" (Collis, "Doctor Who?").

"*Doctor Who* has had many fine actors take the lead, and
several of them danced with greatness, but Capaldi is surely the
greatest actor yet to have been cast as the Doctor, and it's
difficult to imagine the show flailing with this man as its new
face," notes Ross Ruediger in his article, "Why Peter Capaldi Is
the Ideal 12th Doctor." Of course, Capaldi also had a brief
cameo on a *New Who* episode before his casting, just like Karen
Gillan (and in fact, in the same episode). Many fans are
enthusiastic about his portrayal and how he seems to understand
the crux of the science fiction stories:

> In Capaldi's single previous Who outing, "The Fires of
> Pompeii," he was somewhat underused as Caecilius.
> However, look back at that episode and you'll see Capaldi's
> perfect understanding of everything that Doctor Who is
> about near the end of the episode when David Tennant
> steps from the TARDIS to save Caecilius and his family
> from the exploding volcano. The look on Capaldi's face
> when he sees the Doctor – that's it. Right there, in that
> moment, he understands the wonder of the show's
> universe. In hindsight, it's quite the sight to behold.
> (Ruediger)

His journey is yet uncertain, though Moffat has mentioned
that his appearance in "The Fires of Pompeii will actually tie in
(Amy Pond's has not so far, but Freema's early appearance was
attributed to her "cousin" and Wilf, Toshiko, and
Gwen/Gwyneth likewise had their early appearances explained
in the show.)

Other Actors
  ➤ Freema Agyeman had a minor role as Adeola Oshodi, a
    Torchwood employee killed in "Army of Ghosts"
    before becoming Martha Jones. In "Smith and Jones,"
    Martha describes this other character as a deceased
    cousin.

89

- Sir Derek Jacobi (Professor Yana) previously played the Master in *Scream of the Shalka*. Likewise, Geoffrey Beevers (the Master in "The Keeper of Traken") played a character in Seventh Doctor audio adventure "Dust Breeding" who turned out to be the Master in disguise.

- Wilfred Mott's role as the understanding parent who's also a dreamer was meant to be given to Donna's father Geoff, who attends her wedding. When his actor died suddenly, the producers chose to use the newspaperman from "Voyage of the Damned"…and also mention how strange and destiny-filled it is that he and the Doctor keep meeting.

- Helen McCrory is in charge of the convent in "The Vampires of Venice." In another Venetian adventure, she played Casanova's mother…in the Heath Ledger *Casanova,* not the David Tennant one. She also played Narcissa Malfoy in the *Harry Potter* movies but once more missed starring with Tennant.

- Martha's mother, Francine Jones, is played by Adjoa Andoh, who was Sister Jatt in "New Earth."

- David Troughton, son to Second Doctor Patrick Troughton, appeared in "The War Games" in 1969 and "The Curse of Peladon" (1972) before his cameo on 2008 "Midnight."

- A few days after filming "Closing Time," James Corden (playing companion Craig Owens) actually became a father (Hickman 136)

- In the stage play *Doctor Who and the Daleks: Seven Keys to Doomsday*, the companion Jenny is played by Wendy Padbury, Second Doctor companion Zoe Heriot. In the Big Finish version, Jenny's played by Padbury's daughter, Charlie Hayes; the two starred together in several "Companion Chronicles" audios.

- In "The Impossible Astronaut," W. Morgan Sheppard plays older Canton Delaware, and his real-life son Mark Sheppard plays the same character in 1969. They also do this in an episode of *NCIS* ("Broken Bird")

- In "Rise of the Cybermen" Roger Lloyd-Pack plays John Lumic. He played Barty Crouch Sr. in *Harry Potter and the Goblet of Fire,* alongside David Tennant, Barty Crouch Jr.
- The Beast in "The Satan Pit" is voiced by Gabriel Woolf, who played Sutekh in the Fourth Doctor's "Pyramids of Mars."
- The actress for the Plasmavore in "Smith and Jones" played a nurse attacked by vampiric Haemovores in "The Curse of Fenric."
- Many know that Torchwood, an anagram for *Doctor Who* was used as a code word to hide that Russell T Davies was rebooting the series. The tradition continued. Karen Gillan auditioned for Panic Moon, an anagram for companion. Clara's actress Jenna Coleman auditioned for the part of "Men on Waves," which is an anagram for woman seven. Mister Saxon is actually another anagram, for Master No. Six. Astrid is an anagram of TARDIS, but nothing came of this, except that she ends by traveling the stars that are her namesake.
- Jenna Coleman starred in the miniseries *Titanic,* which was scripted by *Downton Abbey* creator Julian Fellowes. She missed the Doctor's Titanic adventure by a few years.
- The little girl in "Castrovalva" is played by Souska John, the niece of Caroline John (Liz Shaw).
- In "The Satan Pit," Mr Jefferson (played by Danny Webb of *Alien³*) appreciates the reference to air-vent escapes. Imitating his previous role, Jefferson buys time for Rose by sacrificing himself in those vents
- Mark Gatiss apparently wrote "The Crimson Horror" for the mother-daughter duo of Dame Diana Rigg and Rachel Stirling. Moffat explains:

> Mark Gatiss, who wrote that episode and who works on Sherlock with me, was appearing in a play with Diana Rigg's daughter, Rachael Stirling, and he said to Rachael, "I think you and your mom

should play the mother and daughter parts in this Doctor Who that I'm writing," and they were up for it. So, it was all down to Mark and his little black book. (Radish, "Steven Moffat Talks Doctor Who")

- In "The Girl Who Waited" Amy mentioned that Rory pretended to be in a band. His actor actually is. In his final appearance, Rory's middle name is revealed as Arthur, just like Arthur Darvill, whose actual first name is Thomas.
- Tosh dies in Jack's arms in "Exit Wounds." John Barrowman and Naoko Mori noted at Comic- Con that they enacted the same scene when they co-starred in *Miss Saigon.*
- *Torchwood's* "Ghost Machine" featured a character named Ed Morgan, played by Gareth Thomas. Morgan's and Thomas's character in *Blake's Seven* had similarly staged suicides, deliberately.
- Richard Dawkins, the famed scientist mentioned in "The Pandorica Opens," is married to Lalla Ward, who played the Doctor's companion Romana. She was previously married to Tom Baker.
- Jo Grant, the companion before Sarah Jane, joined her on her show as did the Eleventh Doctor. The former was skeptical.

> Sarah: "Well, you know he can change his face."
> Jo: "Well I know, but into a baby's?"
> The Doctor: "Oi, imagine it from my point of view! Last time I saw you, Jo Grant, you were, what - 21, 22? It's like someone baked you..." ("The Death of the Doctor")

- In fact, Sladen and Manning's time on Doctor Who was several years before Matt Smith was born.
- Adam's mum is a nurse played by Judy Holt, who played a nurse in *Children's Ward* with the same surname as Adam.

- James Marsters comes to Torchwood in "Kiss Kiss Bang Bang." When he first arrives, he kills a man by lifting him by his throat with super strength and says "Thirsty now." This appears to reference his super-strong vampire character on *Buffy the Vampire Slayer*. He also mentions the Torchwood team needs a blonde.
- In "School Reunion," Anthony Head plays the headmaster (and played Giles on *Buffy the Vampire Slayer*), calls K-9 a "Shooty Dog-thing," using Buffy-style speech patterns. In both shows, he works at an evil school and is one of the few to know what's going on.
- Young Amelia is played by Karen Gillan's real-life cousin Caitlin Blackwood.
- David Tennant dated Sophia Myles (Madame de Pompadour) for two years after their shared episode.
- Clara Oswald may be named after Elisabeth Clara Heath Sladen, who passed away in 2011.
- Eve Myles, who played Gwyneth in "The Unquiet Dead" thrilled Russell T Davies who soon wrote her a part on *Torchwood*. Myles' *Torchwood* character Gwen Cooper is intimated to be related to Gwyneth in "Journey's End" after the Doctor asks Gwen about her family history. Both stories feature the time rift of Cardiff and the character's heroic sacrifice.
- "The Power of Three" sees the return of UNIT, most seen in the Third Doctor's era. Kate Stewart, the Brigadier's daughter, is now running UNIT, following the death of actor Nicholas Courtney in early 2011. Physicist Brian Cox also makes a cameo appearance, theorizing on the origin of the cubes.
- Name gags are played with Ronnie Corbett's character Rani the Slitheen in the Comic Relief minisode "The Two Ranis."
- Richard E. Grant, who plays Dr. Simeon, also played the Doctor in the cartoon Scream of the Shalka. He would have been the official Ninth Doctor had the series not been revived. He also played one of several

Doctors in Doctor Who: The Curse of Fatal Death, written by Steven Moffat.

- Michelle Ryan (Lady Christina de Souza) stated that she is "a huge fan of Doctor Who and [was] very excited to be joining David Tennant and the Doctor Who team." Davies commented that "Michelle is one of the most sought after young actors in the country" and that they were "delighted to announce that she [would] be joining the team" (BBC Press Release).

- Caligula in *I, Claudius* echoes the Master as played by John Simm in the new series. John Simm had already played Caligula and claims he partially based his performance on this. Both characters have an echoing sound in their heads (the sound of drums or Caligula's sound of galloping) and both mock their aged rival.

- When River regenerates, she notes, "I might take the age down a little, just gradually, to freak people out" ("Let's Kill Hitler"). This references the fact that with her episodes shot in reverse her actress is actually getting younger.

- In "Dinosaurs on a Spaceship" Mark Williams who plays Rory's father previously appeared in the Fifth Doctor audio adventure *The Eternal Summer*. Rupert Graves, who plays an Edwardian hunter in this episode, previously worked with Moffat on the BBC series *Sherlock*.

Which Episodes Go Deeper: Self-Reference

References to past episodes and seasons are too numerous to mention – various Doctors meet each other in "The Two Doctors," "The Three Doctors," "The Five Doctors," "Time Crash," and "The Day of the Doctor" (with an homage to these meetings in the misleading "The Next Doctor"). Incidents and past monsters reappear constantly, with Sontarans, Silurians, Daleks, Cybermen, the Great Intelligence, and more in the new series as well as the old. Autons appear in the first episode (though they aren't called that, probably to welcome new fans without cumbersome backstory), beginning a tradition of rewritten monsters and cameos from old favorites

> Moffat is reluctant to plunder Who's history without good reason – "The more you back-reference, the more it feels like a sequel and the sequel is never as good as the original" – but that isn't to say that the past is another galaxy. "Old favorites can return, provided you can do something new and exciting with them. There are no past characters coming back in this series, but I imagine that kids would love to see Captain Jack meet the new Doctor" (McLean).

The show's unreliable canon and lack of a series bible over its long existence (the Daleks, even on the show, have inconsistent abilities and origin stories, for instance) also allows room for *New Who* rewrites and flexibility.

There are many running gags: The constant running, the TARDIS's broken chameleon circuit and wonky steering, the line "it's bigger on the inside," the lack of snow on Christmas each year, and Rory's frequent deaths. The concept of the jaded

Londoners dismissing more and more spectacular alien invasions comes up repeatedly – different companions are different levels of believers, until Amy's crack in time is blamed for some of the forgetfulness. The Londoners at least remember the attacks enough to vacate the city in "Voyage of the Damned," anticipating another apocalypse.

Old Who References in New Who

- The new series plays with the old monsters – Daleks were famed for being unable to climb stairs, as addressed in "Dalek." In the new show, the creatures are restructured to eliminate their humorous weaknesses. (This also occurred in "Remembrance of the Daleks" fifteen years earlier, but viewers were assumed to have forgotten.) Thus the silly plunger is used to crush a man's skull, the Dalek can fly, it can swivel its eyestalk and melt bullets with a forcefield. The decorative spheres are revealed as a terrible self-destruct mechanism. Those who dismissively call it "tinpot" or "pepperpot" soon die horribly.
- On the new show, Cybermen are given a new look (explained by their alternate universe origin) and so are Silurians (explained by their wearing reptilian helmet-masks). The Sontarans still look similar, though the Daleks are "upgraded" through several functions and colors.
- The Doctor's difficulty in remembering the Great Intelligence is a joke-reference to the fact that the Great Intelligence stories have been mostly wiped from the archives. The Doctor also tries to fool the Intelligence by telling it the London Underground in 1967 is a "strategic weakness in metropolitan living." In one Second Doctor episode, the Great Intelligence uses the London Underground in 1967 as a launchpad for its invasion, presumably from this earlier inspiration. That's the catch with time travel.

🎀 Unlike some other returning monsters, the Ice Warriors were not heavily redesigned when they returned in "Cold War." Moffat explained, "With the Ice Warriors, we wanted to create a really good, super-duper version of the one that's already there, rather than changing or revising it" (Radish, "Steven Moffat Talks Doctor Who"). The Ice Warriors appeared alongside the Second Doctor in "The Ice Warriors" (1967) and "The Seeds of Death" (1969) and returned in the Third Doctor stories "The Curse of Peladon" (1972) and "The Monster of Peladon" (1974). Gatiss described "Cold War" as a "love-letter" to the base-under-siege stories that were common during the Second Doctor's era.

🎀 In the minisode "The Great Detective," Vastra and Jenny unknowingly describe the plots of the original series episodes "Spearhead from Space" and "Inferno."

🎀 The Clerics of the Silence use the Greek letter Omega as a symbol, echoing the Time Lord Omega and foretelling River's identity as a part-Time Lord.

🎀 "Rose" is basically a modernized "Spearhead from Space," which introduced the Third Doctor and the Autons, while rebooting the series for color television.

🎀 In "Cold Blood," the Doctor mentions some celery would be really helpful. The Fifth Doctor, after wearing it for years, reveals it can cure Time Lords.

🎀 The Master of the Land of Fiction in the Second Doctor's era is the author of the "Captain Jack Harkaway" stories – Moffat may have invented Captain Jack Harkness as an homage.

🎀 The scene of the Doctor being tortured in "Dalek" resembles the controversial torture scene that opens "Vengeance on Varos." The Doctor raises the controversy by torturing the Dalek in turn.

🎀 In "Image of the Fendahl," The Doctor explains Ma Tyler's "sixth sense" by noting that psychic ability is a common side effect of growing up near a time fissure. This concept is repeated with the psychic abilities of

Gwyneth in "The Unquiet Dead" and Amy's unusual perception

- Donna's Time Beetle recalls the giant spider on Sarah Jane Smith's back in 1974's "Planet of the Spiders."
- In "The Snowmen," the Doctor's ascot and vest evoke the Eighth Doctor. His mangled top hat echoes the one the Second Doctor used to wear, and his fondness for a hook-handled umbrella as a tool echoes the Seventh.
- "The Sontaran Strategem" brings back the Sontarans, as well as a matured Martha Jones and reimagined UNIT. When the Doctor is unsure whether he worked for UNIT in the 70s or 80s, the episode refers to the inconsistencies in dating UNIT stories (unlike in *New Who*, the stories were supposed to be set at a time shortly in the future, with a female prime minister, for instance).
- Clara's headstone in "The Snowmen" states that she was born on 23 November 1866 and that she died on 24 December 1892, meaning she not only shares the same birthday as the show itself but was also 26 years old when she died – the exact same age as *Doctor Who* when it was cancelled.
- In "Day of the Moon" the Doctor and Rory discuss both being present at the Fall of Rome. As an Auton, Rory guarded the Pandorica from the Roman era to the present day, but also the First Doctor set off the Great Fire of Rome in "The Romans."
- When the Master returns, he's developed a taste for jelly babies, like the Fourth Doctor.
- When the Doctor arrives in "The Crimson Horror", he mentions to Clara that he once spent ages trying to get a "gobby Australian" to Heathrow Airport, a reference to the Fifth Doctor's companion Tegan and his efforts to get her back to Heathrow for a multi-episode stretch. The Doctor also uses the phrase "Brave heart, Clara," an expression he often used when talking to Tegan.

➤ Neil Gaiman offers many references in "The Doctor's Wife": The message cube was also seen in "The War Games" – both are disturbing messages from other Time Lords. The makeshift TARDIS control room the Doctor builds from ruined TARDIS pieces echoes the strange styles of control room seen through the previous eras. (The result was designed by the winner of a *Blue Peter* competition.) In both this episode and in "Castrovalva" and "Logopolis," the Doctor jettisons unneeded rooms in exchange for the energy. The Doctor has previously traveled to an alternate universe with only a TARDIS console in "Inferno."

➤ In "The Sound of Drums," U.S. President-Elect Winters states that UNIT protocols for alien first contact were established in 1968; this was the year UNIT entered the series in "The Invasion."

➤ Time Agents from the 51st century are first mentioned in the 1970s episode "The Talons of Weng-Chiang." In her travels, River buys a vortex manipulator like Jack's that used to belong to a Time Agent. When John Hart visits Torchwood, he mentions the Time Agency is all but wiped out.

➤ In "Dalek," "The Time of the Angels," and "The God Complex," alien museums show many old alien friends or their pictures and artifacts. In "The God Complex," the beastly enemy is related to the Nimon, previously a foe in the serial "The Horns of Nimon."

➤ The prison of "Day of the Moon" is made of bricks of dwarf-star alloy, as the ship in "Warriors' Gate," both designed to contain time-sensitives. The Doctor also uses this material to make the chains for the alien father in "The Family of Blood."

➤ Gaiman has stated that the junkyard setting of "The Doctor's Wife" is a deliberate nod back to the first Doctor Who story, "An Unearthly Child," which was initially set in a scrap merchant's yard in Totter's Lane in Shoreditch, London.

- In "Tooth and Claw" the Doctor introduces himself as "James McCrimmon." Jamie McCrimmon was a young Scottish companion of the Second Doctor, and also a reference to David Tennant's Scottish heritage (he even uses his real accent). When Rose encounters the werewolf it says it can see "something of the wolf" in her and that she has "burnt like the Sun," a reference to "The Parting of the Ways."
- In the minisode "Time Crash," The Fifth Doctor bumps into the Tenth. The latter notes:

> You know, I loved being you. Back when I first started, at the very beginning, I was always trying to be old and grumpy and important – like you do, when you're young. And then I was you, and it was all dashing about and playing cricket and my voice going all squeaky when I shouted. I still do that, the voice thing, I got that from you. Oh, and the trainers. And... [putting his glasses on] snap! 'Cos you know what, Doctor? You were my Doctor.

The Fifth Doctor wears his familiar cricket jumper and lapel celery. The Doctors also reminisce about past companions Tegan and Nyssa, as well as the Cybermen, the Mara, the Time Lords' "funny hats" from "Arc of Infinity," and the Master's look during Davison's years.

- In "The Big Bang," the TARDIS protects River by freezing her in a time loop, a surprising reference that seems unforeshadowed. Likewise, the TARDIS's abilities to save old control rooms and transport occupants there or protect itself and offer echoes of the future become sudden plot points in "The Doctor's Wife" and "Journey to the Centre of the TARDIS." This isn't all as sudden as it appears: "Throughout the Classic Series, the TARDIS had a long history of capabilities that got conveniently introduced to serve the plot of one story and were then rarely (or never) mentioned again," critic Steven Cooper explains (172).

- The Ninth Doctor visits the Fourth Great and Bountiful Human Empire (or so he expects) several times. He visited the *Second* Great and Bountiful Human Empire in the First Doctor's "Mission to the Unknown" and "The Daleks' Master Plan."
- Critic Kevin Mahoney deconstructs "The Beast Below," noting:

> To some extent, Moffat also appears to be following Russell T Davies' lead too well, as a similar vessel to the Starship UK formed the basis for Rose's first trip in the TARDIS in 2005's The End of the World…Another Doctor Who story that appears to have influenced Moffat's writing of The Beast Below was Tom Baker's second adventure, "The Ark in Space"….the 1975 production team arguably provided a more convincing image of the future in "The Ark in Space" than the current one (dodgy 1970s coiffures aside). Indeed, although the station and the people within it date from exactly the same time as those on Starship UK (since they too were escaping from the solar flares), their culture is very much different from that depicted in The Beast Below (37-38)

- The head-shaking effect used when the Master transforms humans into the Master Race is a callback to the movie and the Master's special effects in it. In an even more interesting movie moment, the Master taps his fingers a few times in a quick four-drum-beat on arriving at the hospital.
- The Doctor's fez and mop combination of "The Big Bang" nods to "The Silver Nemesis."
- The way the Cybermen in "Army of Ghosts" reveal themselves is a homage to the Cybermen clawing their way out of their pods in "Tomb of the Cybermen."
- That sarcophagus at Torchwood One was seen in "Pyramids of Mars."
- The Doctor and the Master's confrontation in a wasteland during the new series subtly echoes the end of

the old series final episode, "Survival," in which the pair face off on the Cheetah Planet.

➤ "The Impossible Astronaut" offers many references: "The Ambassadors of Death" also features a mysterious astronaut, and "Logopolis" offers a mystery figure in white who brings the Doctor's death. Rory pokes the Doctor in disbelief and asks "How can you be here?" just as the Doctor did to Rory in "The Pandorica Opens." The Astronaut rises out of the lake the way the Dalek famously rises out of the river in "The Dalek Invasion of Earth" or Ace rises out of the lake in "Battlefield." "Brave heart, Canton" is a common Fifth Doctor expression. The TARDIS "decloaking" effect and invisibility were seen in a few old series episodes. Finally, the Doctor notes that "a lot more happens in '69 than anyone remembers." Along with the Silence, this comment references half the year that the viewers don't see and which Amy and company lose most of their memories of. This is even the year Martha and the Tenth Doctor are stuck in the past, and Martha mentions that they went to see the moon landings four times ("Blink"). In addition, the Second Doctor's companions Jaime and Zoe were permanently mindwiped in 1969.

New Who References in New Who

➤ When the Ganger Doctor flashes back through past Doctors in "The Almost People," he mimics the Tenth's voice for a few seconds, then retorts with "Nooo! *Let it go!* We've *MOVED ON!*"

➤ In "The Poison Sky" when UNIT General offers the Tenth Doctor a gas mask, he asks, "Are you my Mummy?"

➤ The Doctor tells the Silence he'll give them a chance to surrender and flee, and then takes it back and adds he's just joking, because it isn't Christmas. This is probably a reference to his actions in "The Christmas Invasion."

🎀 "Waters of Mars" is an anagram of Master of Wars. This appears significant as the Doctor wrestles his god complex and atones for his war in the very next episode.

🎀 In "The Girl Who Waited" older Amy and Rory's conversation as they lean on each side of the TARDIS's door parallels the wall scene between Ten and Rose in "Doomsday," especially given Rory's earlier line, "This isn't fair. You're turning me into you!" Older Amy's line, "Amy Pond in the TARDIS with Rory Williams" also echoes Mickey's "That's the Doctor, in the TARDIS, with Rose Tyler" from "The Age of Steel" (a line also reworked in a deleted scene from "Journey's End").

🎀 Clara discovers that the children she looks after have found historical photographs of her from 1974 ("Hide") and 1983 ("Cold War"). They also found an 1892 photo of her Victorian self ("The Snowmen"), whom they assume to be their Clara.

🎀 The Doctor is held captive in Area 51 in "Day of the Moon," which he had visited previously in the Tenth Doctor animated serial *Dreamland*.

🎀 Christopher Eccleston briefly appears in the line of people becoming converted in "The Age of Steel."

🎀 Wilf's revolver was the same one used by Captain Jack Harkness.

🎀 Davies ends his tenure with Mickey Smith marrying Martha Jones as a nod to "Smith and Jones," Martha's debut adventure.

🎀 Donna and the Doctor have a debate in the Library:

> Donna picks up a book and the Doctor takes it from her.
> DOCTOR: Way-a. Spoilers.
> DONNA: What?

> DOCTOR: These books are from your future. You
> don't want to read ahead. Spoil all the surprises.
> Like peeking at the end.
> DONNA: Isn't travelling with you one big spoiler?
> DOCTOR: I try to keep you away from major plot
> developments. ("Silence in the Library")

This may be a reference to the fact that Donna becomes the most famous woman in the galaxy, with people on distant planets singing songs of her – she might encounter her own biography!

Repeated Arc Words

Series One
The words "bad wolf" appear in dialogue from the Moxx of Balhoon in "The End Of The World," mentioned by Gwyneth in "The Unquiet Dead," as graffiti painted on the TARDIS in "Aliens Of London"/"World War Three," as Henry van Statten's codename in "Dalek," as a TV channel in "The Long Game," scrawled on a poster in "Father's Day," the name of the bomb (in German) in "The Empty Child"/"The Doctor Dances," and the name of nuclear power station (in Welsh) in "Boom Town." Darlig Ulv Stranden, Bad Wolf Bay, is Rose's alt-world weak point between worlds, where she says two goodbyes to the Doctor in Norway.

Series Two
The Torchwood Institute is casually mentioned in "Bad Wolf," "School Reunion," "Rise of the Cybermen," "The Idiot's Lantern," "Love & Monsters," and "Fear Her." The institute creates and fires the weapon of "The Christmas Invasion." It's the agency responsible for the mission to the black hole in "The Impossible Planet"/"The Satan Pit," and is created by Queen Victoria in "Tooth and Claw," before featuring in the two part finale, then recreated as Torchwood Three on the spinoff television show.

Series Three

In 2006's "Love & Monsters," a newspaper headline reads "Saxon Leads Polls with 64 Percent" In "The Runaway Bride," the British military is following Saxon's orders, while his name appears on a news broadcast and election poster in "Smith and Jones." (The poster also appears in the *Torchwood* episode "Captain Jack Harkness.") Agents of Mr Saxon give Francine Jones cryptic warnings in "The Lazarus Experiment" and "42." Meanwhile, the concept of the Doctor turning human with his Time Lord essence in a watch appears in "Human Nature"/"The Family of Blood." With the prophecy of the Face of Boe: "You Are Not Alone," "the stage is set for the three-part finale.

Series Four

In the next year, the planets of the adipose and the Pyroviles vanish. In "Midnight," Dee Dee mentions her paper on the lost moon of Poosh. The honeybees are disappearing. The Master, in mentions the Medusa Cascade. With prophecies such as "There's something on your back" to Donna and "She is coming," referencing Rose Tyler's momentary cameos, the fourth series is exploding with arc references.

In the 2009 specials, "He will knock four times" become the arc words, offered by a human seer in "Planet of the Dead." She adds: "[Gallifrey] is returning. It is returning through the dark, and then Doctor... oh but then... he will knock four times." Characters in "Planet of the Ood" and "The Wedding of Sarah Jane Smith" mention the Doctor's upcoming fate. In "The Waters of Mars," the Doctor thunders that an alien adversary won't get to knock more than three times and tries to alter a fixed point, but fails. When "The End of Time" finally comes, the Master's four-beat sound in his head appears to be the four knocks. However, the Doctor survives the Time Lord invasion and saves the day, only to hear Wilfred knocking to be let out. Four times. The Doctor sacrifices himself, then bids goodbye to all the Davies-era companions, along with the Davies era itself, bookending the show.

105

Series Five

For the fifth series, the crack on Amy's wall is the "arc image," appearing in every episode. The issues of Amy and Rory's abandoned wedding, then her forgetting Rory get a nod in each episode. River Song also mentions that the Pandorica adventure is coming soon as she leaves in "Flesh and Stone." The two-part finale acts as a sequel to every single series five episode: Vincent van Gogh ("Vincent and the Doctor") has a premonition, which he paints and delivers to Winston Churchill ("Victory of the Daleks"), who sends it to Liz Ten's art gallery ("The Beast Below"), and calls River Song ("The Time of Angels"), who finally delivers it. Rory, lost in "Cold Blood," reappears, as does Young Amelia from "The Eleventh Hour" and finally Amy and Rory's wedding takes place.

Combining the plot of the Pandorica with the following year's Silence, Prisoner Zero tells the Doctor that "The universe is cracked. The Pandorica will open. Silence will fall" in "The Eleventh Hour." The Silence's ship (seen in "The Lodger") also returns the following year.

The Doctor's enemies in the Series Five finale episode include just about every new series prosthetic alien (as old series ones and more complex creatures like the Atraxi would have required more work): Judoon ("Smith and Jones"), Hoix ("Love & Monsters"), Silurians ("The Hungry Earth"), Robo-forms ("The Christmas Invasion"), Uvodni (*The Sarah Jane Adventures*: "Warriors of Kudlak"), and Blowfish (*Torchwood*: "Kiss Kiss Bang Bang"), as well as Daleks, Cybermen, and Sontarans. *Doctor Who Confidential* notes that this many different monsters had never before been seen side by side. River describes the ships overhead as Daleks, Cybermen, Sontarans, Terileptils ("The Visitation"), Slitheen ("Aliens of London"), Nestene ("Rose"), Drahvin ("Galaxy Four"), Sycorax ("The Christmas Invasion"), Zygons ("Terror of the Zygons"), Atraxi ("The Eleventh Hour"), Draconians ("Frontier in Space"), and even Chelonians (from the novel *The Highest Science*), and Haemo-Goths (from the novel *The Forgotten Army*).

106

Series Six

Series Six begins with the Doctor's death in "The Impossible Astronaut." *Who* writer Gareth Roberts notes a theme of "death and lingering darkness" through the sixth series ("Open All Hours"). As he adds, "Time is closing in on him and he can't put off going to Lake Silencio and his doom" ("An Interview with Gareth Roberts"). The phrase "silence will fall" mirrors the inevitable death, though ironically, silence will only fall if the Doctor lives. Through the many revelations about River Song as they fall in love in the wrong order, the Doctor learns of his upcoming death and tries to escape the inevitable. In the process, the Doctor spends two hundred years seeing the universe and waving to his friends from the history books. As the Doctor puts it:

> Been knocking about. A bit of a farewell tour. Things to do, people to see. There's always more. I could invent a new color, save the Dodo, join the Beatles...For me, it never stops. Liz the First is still waiting in a glade to elope with me. I could help Rose Tyler with her homework. I could go on all of Jack's stag parties in one night. ("The Wedding of River Song")

As his arc ends in "Night Terrors," "Closing Time," and "The Wedding of River Song," creepy children sing foreboding nursery rhymes, heralding the Doctor's fate. In this series, the mysterious face looking at Amy and the revelation that she's a type of ganger are tied to River's birth, of course. There are more reunions: "A Good Man Goes to War" unites the pirates, Danny Boy, Dorium, Madame Vastra, Jenny, Strax, and all the Doctor's allies. Rory even dresses as a Roman. On the opposite side are clerics, Cybermen, headless monks, and endless soldiers.

"The Wedding of River Song" features Churchill and Dickens in the out-of-time universe, along with Daleks, pterodactyls (*Torchwood:* "Everything Changes"), Cleopatra ("The Pandorica Opens"), the Teselecta ("Let's Kill Hitler"), Silurians ("Cold Blood"), and Dorium ("A Good Man Goes to War"). Amy sketches her past adventures: Daleks, Silurians, vampires, pirates, and Weeping Angels. River also recruits everyone in the universe to help, saying, "The sky is full of a million, million voices saying yes, of course we'll help. You've touched so many lives, saved so many people. Did you think when your time came, you'd really have to do more than just ask? You've decided that the universe is better off without you, but the universe doesn't agree." This episode bookends events of all the River Song episodes, especially "Forest of the Dead," "The Impossible Astronaut," and "A Good Man Goes to War," while setting up Trenzalore and the question that will provide the next year's arc.

Series Seven
Series Seven guides viewers through Rory and Amy's balancing a normal life with their Doctor adventures, then Clara's short arc as the Eleventh Doctor's Impossible Girl. The latter offers her favorite expressions and talismans: soufflés, "Run, you clever boy and remember," and her parents' special leaf, along with her jobs as governess and protector. Trenzalore and the adventures of Vastra's Victorian team continue through the series, all culminating in "The Name of the Doctor."

The Expanded Universe Appears in Canon

With fifty years to write (and some of those years with no episodes whatsoever), the expanded universe as it's called has flourished. There are comic books, comic strips in *Doctor Who Magazine,* two series of independent novels, and an extensive series of audio adventures, these latter starring most original Doctors and companions as voice actors. The canonicity (i.e. whether these episodes count as really having happened to the television Doctor) is debatable.

> In the Bizarro World of science fiction canon there is a curious reversal, whereby audiovisual narratives are accorded greater precedence than prose, or indeed audio material featuring the same cast as the original television incarnation. Wood and Miles describe such material as

"secondary sources," whereas the television series is presented as "The 'truth' about the Doctor Who universe." (Harvey 33).

Most of these novels play with the material in the episodes, as the Doctor uses the incorrect eighties slang that Ace used on the show, or fill in the missing moments between episodes. Most novels along with the popular Cloister Library and Discontinuity Guide online attempt to make all the adventures, on and off screen work together as canon, explaining discrepancies through lies, memory loss, or the ever-popular rewriting of time. *Doctor Who: A History of the Universe* by *Who* novelist Lance Parkin attempts to accept all events as canon and place them on a solid timeline – the complete history of the *Doctor Who* universe, from the creation to the end of the universe billions of years in the future.

> Intriguingly, the short story "The Five O'Clock Shadow" by Nev Fountain, which appears in *Short Trips: A Day in the Life*, attempts to incorporate the Cushing films [made in the Sixties and not considered canon, as they rewrite and recast events of the show] into the official continuity by suggesting that the characters from the movies are figments of the real Doctor's imagination, brought about as a means of defeating a foe. This is a further role of spin-off media: the ability to seal up holes in continuity, to effectively shore up the overarching mythology. (Harvey 34).

Nonetheless, *New Who* occasionally references the books, comics, and audio adventures, bolstering their existence as part of canon. Neil Gaiman notes, for instance:

> There's nothing to say that Moffat can't or won't use ideas from novels, of course. He's done it before. The first half-dozen episodes of Series 6 had a companion (Amy) animating an artificial copy of herself while her real body was kept dormant. That bears a suspicious resemblance to what happened to Ace in the 1993 novel, *Shadowmind*, but with several changes: Ace knew what was going on, Amy didn't; with Ace, it was done to assist the Doctor but, with

Amy, the purpose was hostile to him; & so on. ("Q & A: Neil Gaiman")

Many other examples of novel or audio adventures concepts appear on the show, lending credibility to the beloved fan works.

- Most famously, "Human Nature" is a rewrite of a Seventh Doctor novel with the same plot (admittedly suggesting the books may not be canon after all, as the adventure wouldn't have happened twice).
- In an issue of *Doctor Who Magazine*, Susan's Gallifreyan name is revealed as Arkytior, meaning "rose." Rose Tyler may be named in homage to her.
- The *Torchwood* episode "Reset" has Martha Jones use the alias Samantha ("Sam") Jones, a companion from the BBC Books Eighth Doctor Adventures.
- The Doctor references the (not canon) stage play *Doctor Who and the Daleks in the Seven Keys to Doomsday* when he mentions he loves the Time Lord fairytale "Snow White and the Seven Keys To Doomsday" in "Night Terrors."
- In *Remembrance of the Daleks,* the Dalek Emperor disguise worn by Davros is based on the Emperor of the Dalek Chronicles comic, not the Emperor of the TV series.
- "Dalek" rewrote elements of the Big Finish audio drama *Jubilee.* The "Jubilee Pizza" box added in homage was cut from the script, but appeared in a few episodes of *Torchwood.*
- One of the vendors in "The Long Game" sells "kronkburgers" from the *Doctor Who Magazine* comic strip "The Iron Legion."
- The term "rel" as a Dalek unit of time was first used in the Peter Cushing movies. It appeared in some Expanded Universe stories, and then finally became official in "Doomsday."
- The episode "Bad Wolf" mentions Lucifer, echoing the Doctor Who New Adventures novel *Lucifer Rising* by Andy Lane and Jim Mortimore, and in "Doomsday" the

Doctor mentions Arcadia, from the New Adventures novel *Deceit* by Peter Darvill-Evans.

●○ In "The Impossible Astronaut"/"Day of the Moon," like Eighth Doctor novel *Alien Bodies*, one of the TARDIS crew jumps off a tall building and relies on the TARDIS being in the right place and time to catch them. *Alien Bodies* also shows the Doctor's body being bought and sold, something feared in this episode.

●○ New Earth is described as the fifteenth New Earth, possibly a reference to the many different New Earths of the books.

●○ The numbered mood patches of "Gridlock" parallel the number coded mood controllers in the Ninth Doctor novel *Only Human* by TV writer Gareth Roberts.

●○ The banana-switched-for-gun gag actually started in the Eighth Doctor Adventures, before the Steven Moffat's episodes "The Empty Child"/"The Doctor Dances," "The Girl in the Fireplace," and "Let's Kill Hitler."

●○ The Brigadier's daughter, Kate Stewart, appears from the Expanded Universe onto the episode "The Power of Three."

●○ "Are you my mummy?" echoes the "are you my father?" repeat words from Steven Moffat's favorite Sixth Doctor story, "The Holy Terror" by Big Finish.

●○ "Utopia" echoes much of the Big Finish adventure *Master.*

●○ "The Shakespeare Code's" Queen Elizabeth I cameo was written into the story at Davies' request, inspired by Roberts' Sixth Doctor Big Finish adventure *The One Doctor.*

●○ "The Doctor's Wife" is not the first time that a TARDIS has taken the form of a woman within the Doctor Who universe, as Laurence Miles' *Alien Bodies* uses this concept and in his novel *Interference*, one of the Doctor's companions, Compassion, transforms into a TARDIS.

111

- The TARDIS appearing in a human form and the possessed TARDIS harassing its occupants echo events of the Big Finish audio *Zagreus*, as well as the comic series *The Forgotten*.
- Martha asks the Doctor if he's got a brother when they first meet, and he replies – "No, not anymore; just me." In fact, the Doctor's brother, Braxiatel, is a character in the Eighth Doctor Bernice Summerfield stories.
- The Doctor's description of the "Could-Have-Been King with his army of Meanwhiles and Never-Weres" who fought in the Time War ("The End of Time") may be a nod to the Doctor Who Expanded Universe, and specifically the Faction Paradox.
- Yvonne Hartman in "Army of Ghosts" is a combination of Yvonne Hartley and Doctorman Allan, from Big Finish's Cybermen origin story, *Spare Parts*. In it, the Fifth Doctor and Nyssa visit the "Tenth Planet," Mondas. Though the planet is dying, Nyssa befriends the young woman Yvonne Hartley. The Mondasians' survival suits are the first Cybermen exteriors, invented by Doctorman Allan. The Doctor tries to prevent the rise of the Cybermen, but is unsuccessful.
- As the Eighth Doctor regenerates, he salutes his past companions from the audio adventures McGann voiced, establishing them as canon: "Charley [Pollard], C'rizz, Lucie [Miller], Tamsin [Drew], Molly [O'Sullivan]" ("The Night of the Doctor").

Torchwood, Sarah Jane, and Who

The word Torchwood is an anagram for Doctor Who and was used by Davies to hide the fact that he was planning a Who reboot. In series two, Torchwood becomes the Doctor's nemesis, though it becomes an ally under Captain Jack's control. Eventually, *Torchwood* becomes its own edgier TV show, mirroring *Doctor Who* just as its name does (the Doctor never has a cameo there, mainly to discourage younger fans from tuning in).

While *New Who* introduces classic monsters as if they're new and doesn't demand viewers be familiar with the original series, *The Sarah Jane Adventures* often nods to old series Sarah Jane episodes and *New Who* as well. The Doctor himself is often mentioned, as are the gun-toting commandos of Torchwood and UNIT, whom Sarah Jane doesn't want to involve. Nonetheless, Sarah Jane remembers the Doctor's lessons and mimics them, while also forming her own morality. "Captain Jack and Sarah Jane Smith lead their teams according to (most of the time!) their new moral values caused by rising above one's self in *Torchwood* and *The Sarah Jane Adventures,* without recourse to the Doctor" (Deller 245). Sarah Jane mentions "Slitheen in Downing Street" and the Cup of Athelstan, suggesting she's keeping track of incidents involving the Doctor.

Photos of the Brigadier and other UNIT personnel appear in the first episode, and the Sontarans are mentioned in "The Eye of the Gorgon" before they appear in *Doctor Who*'s "The Sontaran Stratagem." Later, Sarah Jane mentions the ATMOS incident. Sarah Jane lives on Bannerman Road, referencing the old episode "Delta and the Bannermen." Further, "The Mad Woman in the Attic" offers flashbacks to Sarah Jane's days with the Third and Fourth Doctors.

Of course, the Tenth Doctor famously drops in to stop Sarah Jane's wedding (he also gives her young friends a TARDIS ride, making them technically his companions). "Death of the Doctor" welcomes the Eleventh Doctor and former Third Doctor companion Jo Grant in one episode and the beloved Brigadier in another – *The Sarah Jane Adventures* has more old series companions guest star than *New Who* does. In a delightful fannish moment, Sarah Jane also mentions what many of the twentieth-century companions are up to decades later, in a way never addressed on the original series. She explains:

> I can't be sure, but there's a woman called Tegan in Australia, fighting for Aboriginal rights. There's a Ben and Polly, in India, running an orphanage there. There was Harry. Oh, I loved Harry. He was a doctor. He did such good work with vaccines. He saved thousands of lives. And

113

there's a Dorothy something. She runs that company, A Charitable Earth [clearly Ace, especially with her company's acronym]. She's raised billions. And this couple in Cambridge, both professors. Ian and Barbara Chesterton. Rumor has it, they've never aged. Not since the sixties. I wonder. ("The Death of the Doctor")

With Jo's adventures across the world and many children, and the Brigadier's last hurrah, Sarah Jane's series caps the old series better than the Doctor does. It also enjoys nodding to the franchise in subtler ways, as does *Torchwood:*

- Sarah Jane's newspaper clipping in SJA: "Lost in Time" is dated November 23rd, 47 years to the day after *Doctor Who* premiered.
- SJA: "The Vault of Secrets" has Sarah Jane and Mr Smith stopping a NASA rover from spotting some of the "Pyramids of Mars," (from the original series Sarah Jane episode of that name), and she meets the Alliance of Shades from the animated serial *Dreamland.*
- The Trickster, a specifically Sarah Jane villain, is mentioned on *Torchwood* and *New Who* but doesn't appear there. Creatures from the Trickster's Brigade, like the bug on Donna's back, appear in both other series.
- During the *Torchwood* episode "Captain Jack Harkness," Vote Saxon signs appear on a door and there's Bad Wolf graffiti in the abandoned hospital.

What's Happening in the World:
Pop Culture References

The series has so many pop culture references, it would almost easier to list the ones *not* present. The Doctor tries a Wii, compares himself to Gandalf and Mary Poppins, tries not to spoil the seventh *Harry Potter* book. On *The Sarah Jane Adventures,* Clyde in particular is a pop culture fiend, eagerly gushing about his favorite comics and computer games. The series keeps itself fresh by acknowledging its surrounding culture, all the while paying homages to its many inspirations, particularly in science fiction.

Science Fiction

Technobabble (convincing science dialogue like 'reverse the neutron flow") is a science fiction staple. The Doctor subverts this in "Blink," then commonly after as he says, "[Time is] a ball of wibbly-wobbly Timey Wimey...stuff...it sort of got away from me, yeah" and "This is my Timey Wimey Detector. It goes 'ding' when there's stuff." Though he writes science fiction, Moffat dislikes technobabble, and thus uses "timey-wimey" explanations and metaphors. Occasionally he calls attention to this preference – for instance, in "A Christmas Carol" while the Doctor's trying to scientifically explain why flying fish like Abigail's singing, a fish bites him. He gives up. ("Look, the fish like singing, now shut up!")

"Science fiction provides scenarios of alternative futures and encourages thinking through various scenarios...science fiction is imaginative in the sense that possibilities for interaction and the politics of encounter can be drawn out and studied" (Dixit

115

292). By examining concepts from alienness to the harm of technology, characters and viewers can explore these issues on earth.

Further, the companions on *New Who* aren't idiots – they've seen science fiction shows and know how they work (thank goodness!). This of course leads to dialogue spiced with familiar references:

> MICKEY: But if the date's the same, it's parallel, right? Am I right? Like a parallel Earth where they've got Zeppelins. Am I right? I'm right, aren't I?
> DOCTOR: Must be.
> ROSE: So, a parallel world where –
> MICKEY: Oh, come on. You've seen it on films. Like an alternative to our world where everything's the same but a little bit different, like, I don't know, traffic lights are blue, Tony Blair never got elected. ("Rise of the Cybermen")

The Doctor must regretfully tell Mickey that bouncing off to alternate realities isn't as easy as it looks on television…or at least it isn't anymore.

> MICKEY: But I've seen it in comics. People go hopping from one alternative world to another. It's easy.
> DOCTOR: Not in the real world. It used to be easy. When the Time Lords kept their eye on everything, you could hop between realities, home in time for tea. Then they died, and took it all with them. The walls of reality closed, the worlds were sealed. Everything became that bit less kind. ("Rise of the Cybermen")

In "The Shakespeare Code," Martha's first time travel trip, she asks numerous genre-savvy questions. There are several references to the paradoxes of time travel: Martha mentions the possibility of killing her grandfather, an allusion to the grandfather paradox, when she first steps from the TARDIS. She also suggests that stepping on a butterfly might change the future of the human race, an idea that originates in Ray Bradbury's short story "A Sound of Thunder." The Doctor in turn explains how history could be changed with devastating results by referencing *Back to the Future.*

Terry Nation, the man who invented the Daleks back in 1963 and wrote many of the Dalek episodes that followed, wrote a great deal for other cult science fiction shows. He created series like *Survivors* and *Blake's 7,* series which are still influencing culture – *Survivors* was back on the small screen as recently as 2010 and *Blake's 7* still has audio stories and books being made. Alwyn Turner, author of a new autobiography about Nation titled *The Man Who Invented the Daleks* explains:

> And, of course, the greatest survivors of all are the Daleks. They've been around for nearly half a century now and they show no signs of going away. There are young kids coming to them now who are as captivated as their grandparents were back in the 1960s. When Nation sat down to knock out that first Daleks story in 1963 – rushing through the assignment in a week in order to get back to what he considered proper writing – he tapped into his own love of adventure stories and pulp science-fiction and conjured up an enduring myth. How these things happen is always a mystery, but their instant resonance can't be denied...Daleks are the single most enduring creations of British television in the 20th century. It's a bold claim but I really can't think of any rivals. The Daleks were created specifically for the screen – rather than being adapted from literature – and their continuing appeal is not dependent on any specific writers or actors; they exist simply as themselves. (Cawley, "Alwyn Turner on Terry Nation")

Star Trek

◖◗ *Doctor Who: The Writer's Tale*, written by Davies and Benjamin Cook, reveals Davies' eagerness for the Doctor to journey where no man has gone before...back in 2004, a *Doctor Who/Star Trek* crossover was seriously on his list of plans, until *Enterprise* was canceled. One idea for the 2009 Easter Special was a *Star Trek* pastiche, with the Doctor mocking something quite like the Enterprise – "The Doctor on board the

Enterprise, puncturing all that Starfleet pomposity with this sheer Doctor-ness."

◀ In "The Empty Child" Rose introduces the Doctor as "Mr. Spock." Captain Jack, from the 51st century, doesn't recognize the reference. Writer Steven Moffat says in the DVD commentary that Rose was supposed to ask "Doctor who?" with the Doctor breaking the fourth wall and saying, "I'd rather have *Doctor Who* than *Star Trek*." The following line in the next episode subverts the *Star Trek* tagline of a mission to "seek out new life and new civilizations":

> DOCTOR: So many species, so little time.
> ROSE: What is that what we do when we get out there? We seek out new life and...and...
> DOCTOR: Dance. ("The Doctor Dances")

◀ The nanogenes of "The Doctor Dances" were originally called "nanites" but this was changed because of concerns about the same term's usage in the *Star Trek* franchise.

◀ The Tenth Doctor's death from radiation poisoning while sealed in a glass chamber echoes *Star Trek II: The Wrath of Khan*.

◀ Alt-universe stories were relatively unusual at the time of the Third Doctor's "Inferno" (though it was filmed after Star Trek's "Mirror Mirror"). Now all the science fiction shows have them. The Doctor has visited alt-universes a few times since, particularly to "Pete's world" where Rose is finally abandoned.

◀ The *Doctor Who* television movie instead of saying chameleon circuit says the *Star Trek* term cloaking device.

◀ Some fans comment that the *Star Trek: The Next Generation*'s Borg are clearly derived from the Cybermen. In "The Pandorica Opens," a Cyberman actually uses the Borg catchphrase, "You will be assimilated."

- "We don't need any *Star Trek* gadgets," Clyde complains, eyeing Sarah Jane's sonic lipstick in "Eye of the Gorgon" part 2.
- The comic miniseries *Star Trek: The Next Generation/Doctor Who: Assimilation²* (2012) from IDW is a crossover of *Star Trek: The Next Generation* and *Doctor Who*. As the Borg and the Cybermen ally, The Eleventh Doctor, Rory, and Amy must struggle to stop them along with the Enterprise crew. There's a cyber-borg controller, the Doctor's babble bothers Worf, and everyone's acting true to form.
- The forehead to forehead memory sharing seems to mimic mind melds – and spoofs it when the Doctor produces the same effect by headbutting Craig in "The Lodger." In that episode, while talking to an emergency hologram, the Doctor delivers a deadpan "Please state the nature of the emergency," the Doctor's tagline on *Star Trek: Voyager*.

Star Wars
- The John Hart hologram on *Torchwood's* "Kiss Kiss Bang Bang" facetiously pleads: "Help me Obi-Wan Kenobi, you're my only hope!"
- "Enemy of the Bane" contains a clear reference as the vicious Mrs. Wormwood cries, "Luke. I am your Mother!"
- River's costume in "The Big Bang" was intended to resemble the costumes of Princess Leia and Han Solo blended together, so she appeared like a "female Han Solo," according to the audio commentary.
- River negotiates with a blue-skinned merchant to obtain a vortex manipulator, evoking tough Han Solo once again.
- Clyde was once upset that his history teacher didn't accept the battle of Hoth as fact.
- "Last time I was sentenced to death, I ordered four hyper-vodkas for my breakfast. All a bit of a blur after

that. Woke up in bed with both my executioners. Lovely couple. They stayed in touch. Can't say that about most executioners" ("The Doctor Dances"). Critics describe Jack Harkness as "a little bit Han Solo, a little bit Jack Sparrow, with a touch of Tom Cruise" (McFarland).

●◀ The alien planet Clara visits in "The Rings of Akhaten" has about fifty alien species mixing and is thus reminiscent of the *Star Wars* cantina. The scene in which the Tenth Doctor bids farewell to Jack before his death is an even more similar alien watering hole.

●◀ The Master's lightning bolts resemble Darth Vader's.

●◀ "Help us, Doctor, you're our only hope," people say in "The Beast Below."

●◀ In "Victory of the Daleks," the Spitfires-in-space scene felt *Star Wars*-like to some viewers (though this scene was in turn inspired by the movie *The Dambusters*. In the same episode, a man is revealed to be a robot when his robotic right hand is sliced off.

●◀ The Eleventh Doctor tells Amy he's like, "I dunno, Gandalf! A space Gandalf. Or the little green one in *Star Wars*." He makes a lightsaber noise to illustrate his point and fend off an amorous Amy in the minisode after "Flesh and Stone."

●◀ Steven Moffat has been nicknamed "The Moff" and "The Grand Moff" by fans as well as by Russell T Davies.

●◀ Jamie and Zoe's spacesuits in "The Wheel in Space" were actually used in the original trilogy (most noticeably by Bossk the Bounty Hunter).

●◀ In the novel Mission: Impractical, the Sixth Doctor and Frobisher attend the American premiere of Star Wars at Mann's Chinese Theatre. The Doctor notes that actor Peter Cushing (who played Grand Moff Tarkin) looks familiar, an in-joke as Cushing had played the film version of the Doctor in the 1960s.

●◀ In the novels and comics, Eighth Doctor companions Sam Jones, Izzy Sinclair, and Fitz Kreiner are fans. The latter sees all nine *Star Wars* films at a cinema in the 2040s.

- Meanwhile, Clyde on *The Sarah Jane Adventures* calls Luke his "young padawan" in several episodes.
- The Tenth Doctor mentions that in *Star Wars* and his own life, ventilation ducts never seem to work out (*Dreamland*).
- Behind the scenes, Russell T Davies was asked to write for *Star Wars: The Clone Wars,* and on that show David Tennant voiced the droid character Huyang.

More Science Fiction

- The Tenth Doctor feels like Arthur Dent from *Hitchhiker's Guide* (whom he says he's met) when he adventures in a bathrobe in "The Christmas Invasion." In fact, Douglas Adams was a long-time writer of the classic *Who* episodes. The episode "Shada" by Douglas Adams, included a Nutrimat drinks machine and a Ford Prefect car, both references to *The Hitchhiker's Guide to the Galaxy.*
- In "Destiny of the Daleks," episode 1, by Terry Nation (with Douglas Adams as script editor at the time), the Fourth Doctor reads a book by Oolong Caloophid, author of *Where God Went Wrong, More of God's Greatest Mistakes* and *That About Wraps it up for God Then* in Adams' *Hitchhikers Guide.*
- Science fiction writer Neil Gaiman notes that the scenes of Amy and Rory running through the TARDIS in "The Doctor's Wife" are a "very intentional" reference to Harlan Ellison's "I Have No Mouth and I Must Scream" (Cawley).
- Like *Firefly, Battlestar Galactica,* and *Babylon 5, New Who* is the story of a war's aftermath, not a war – the Daleks and Time Lords had their colossal battle and all that remains is to rebuild the Doctor's mission during the "Galactic Recession" of the Ninth Doctor's travels.

- *Doctor Who*'s format, according to James Chapman, "places it directly in the historical lineage of British literary science fiction," in the vein of H.G. Wells' *The Time Machine* (5).
- Another critic adds, *"Doctor Who* follows other literary motifs found in Wells' *The War of the Worlds* (1898), specifically that of alien invasion" (Geraghty 86).
- K-9 arrived before R2-D2 but stands alongside other popular robot sidekicks: Twiki *(Buck Rogers in the 25*[th] *Century), Metal Mickey,* and Muffit *(Battlestar Galactica)*.
- The matrix, a shared telepathic world of imagination appeared in the old *Who* series long before the movie *The Matrix*.
- Gwen's old partner, Andy, calls Jack Harkness "Mulder" on occasion.
- Moffat describes the Silence calling them "A bit like the greys, a bit like Munch's The Scream" (Hickman 43)
- Donna references *Journey to the Centre of the Earth* when she seeks the Empress of the Racnoss under her building in "The Runaway Bride." This seminal work of science fiction created many famous tropes, and also inspired the title of "Journey to the Centre of the Tardis."
- Cyborgs possibly inspired by the original cybermen include the replicants in *Blade Runner, RoboCop, Terminator, Star Trek's* Borg, and the entire Cyberpunk genre, especially William Gibson's *Neuromancer* (1984). "James Chapman traces the Cybermen's cultural and scientific ancestry as far back as Mary Shelley's *Frankenstein* (1818), with its notion of replacing human body parts, to *Metropolis* and *The Day the Earth Stood Still* (1951), with their depictions of metallic cyborgs and androids" (Geraghty 89).
- There are several worlds reminiscent of the novel *1984* – dystopias where people are always being watched. "The Beast Below" offers one, as does the world of "The Long Game"…which even has a Big Brother

house. The Sixth Doctor, upon arriving in that year, claims that 1984 was "never as good as the book" (*The Reaping*).

- On *Dreamland,* the Tenth Doctor felt sad that Cassie and Jimmy hadn't seen *Alien.* Toshiko Sato in turn compared a body with its heart ripped out to "that bit in *Alien* where that thing bursts out of John Hurt." (TW: "Greeks Bearing Gifts")

Fantasy
Harry Potter

- Davies actually contacted Harry Potter author JK Rowling, asking her to write for the show, but she declined the invitation because she was too busy (as mentioned in *Doctor Who: The Writer's Tale*).
- Martha uses the Harry Potter spell "Expelliarmus" to banish the Shakespearean witches and she and the Doctor discuss the (then unpublished) seventh book.

> MARTHA: So, magic and stuff. That's a surprise. It's all a little bit Harry Potter.
> DOCTOR: Wait till you read book seven (published 2007). Oh, I cried. ("The Shakespeare Code")

- Many Harry Potter actors have joined the show, like David Tennant (Barty Crouch Jr.) and Michael Gambon in "A Christmas Carol" (Dumbledore). "Dinosaurs on a Spaceship" features Mr. Weasley as Rory's dad and David Bradley (Argus Filch) as the space pirate.
- When planning "The Next Doctor," Davies considered a fantastical adventure in which JK Rowling would appear as herself (an idea never fully enacted).
- The Master returns when his followers willingly sacrifice themselves and his old nemesis (his wife) unwillingly sacrifices part of herself. This, together with his skeletal visage caught between life and death echoes Voldemort's return.

123

- "The Parting of the Ways" is a chapter title in *Harry Potter and the Goblet of Fire*.
- Tennant's Hogwarts robes go by briefly as he seeks his Tenth Doctor look.
- With "Tooth and Claw," the Mill was eager animate a werewolf, having already made such a creature for *Harry Potter and The Prisoner of Azkaban*.

More Fantasy

- "What do you keep in here? Why have you got zombie creatures? Good guys do not have zombie creatures. Rule one basic storytelling," Clara tells the Doctor ("Journey to the Centre of the Tardis").
- In "New Earth," Rose refers to Chip as "Gollum." In "Last of the Time Lords," the Master calls the Doctor Gandalf.
- River notes, "I hate good wizards in fairy tales. They always turn out to be him [the Doctor]." ("The Pandorica Opens")
- In a hilarious extra scene from *The Brilliant Book 2012*, the Eleventh Doctor appears as the king's fool in "Humpty Dumpty." He saves the egg-shaped hero, and announces, "I've saved you from death so we must face the facts/You are now in my debt and I've work for you, Strax." (Hickman 29).
- A few episodes are given an epic or fairytale theme with the opening and closing narration, particularly "Doomsday," "Forest of the Dead," "The Eleventh Hour," "The Angels Take Manhattan," and "The Name of the Doctor."
- In the comic *Doctor Who: A Fairytale Life*, a four-issue IDW Publishing miniseries featuring the Eleventh Doctor, the Doctor takes Amy to a world of fairies and unicorns on a recreation planet...and she ends up the damsel in distress. As always occurs, the perfect planet is actually flawed – in this case, filled with a series of

mysterious kidnappings as characters are being whisked off to a dread tower.

➤ Neil Gaiman's "The Doctor's Wife" uses the unusual word petrichor as a password, meaning the smell of dust after rain. ("Closing Time" has Amy Pond name a new perfume after this word as well).

> The word 'petrichor' has a peculiar etymology. Although it's derived from the Greek for "stone" and "blood of the gods," it's not an ancient word at all, since two Australian scientists first devised it in 1964...[Famed British fantasy writer] Terry Pratchett used this term in his 1998 Australian satire *The Last Continent*. The next author to notice this word and to popularise it was Neil Gaiman (scriptwriter of "The Doctor's Wife") in his 2001 novel *American Gods*. It's not too surprising that Neil Gaiman would devour and take inspiration from Terry Pratchett's work in this way, since they co-wrote *Good Omens* in 1990. (Cooper 2011, 228)

➤ The Doctor refers to the Master as Skeletor in "The End of Time." He certainly looks it...

➤ The 23rd of November and 1963 are referenced constantly on the show as the premier of the first episode. However, there are additional meanings to that time:

> The day before the first ever episode of Doctor Who was broadcast on British television - the 22nd of November 1963 - is etched into world history forever due to the assassination of John F. Kennedy. However, that day was also notable for the deaths of a pair of celebrated British authors. One was Aldous Huxley, and the other was C.S. Lewis - who therefore missed by the narrowest of margins the chance to see a science fiction twist on the enchanted wardrobe from his famous Narnia books that opened onto whole worlds of adventure. The similarities between Lewis's magic wardrobe and the TARDIS have often been noted,

> especially by current Doctor Who showrunner Steven Moffat, and in this year's Christmas special he uses *The Lion, the Witch and the Wardrobe* as inspiration for a festive bit of escapism. (Cooper 2011, 228)

🎀 The Narnia adaptation "The Doctor, the Widow and the Wardrobe" has only a mild connection with the original material, though it features the TARDIS as wardrobe, a familiar looking snowy wonderland, and two children banished from London for the war. In the comic *The Professor, the Queen and the Bookshop*, C.S. Lewis is inspired to turn Amy and Rory's adventure into the Narnia books.

🎀 There is a short series of H.P. Lovecraft and *Doctor Who* crossovers featuring Azathoth, the Gods of Ragnarok, Cthulhu, and Dagon, the Great Old Ones who originated out of the Cthulhu Mythos based on Lovecraft's work: the novels *White Darkness*, *All-Consuming Fire* and *Millennial Rites*. Much effort is made to integrate Lovecraft's Old Ones into the existing Doctor Who episodes, as the Doctor explains:

> The Great Old Ones are these gods. There's Cthulhu, who we met in Haiti…and the Gods of Ragnarok…and Nyarlathotep, who I sincerely hope never to encounter. And Dagon, who was worshipped by the Sea Devils, and the entity known as Hastur the Unspeakable who also goes around calling himself Fenric…and Yog-Sothoth, who I met in Tibet and again in London, and Lloigor, who settled quite happily on Vortis…oh, there's a lot of them. All alien to this universe and its laws, both moral and physical. (*All-Consuming Fire* 221)

In the original episodes, Sutekh (partly based on the Egyptian god Seth) and the Fendahl, show Lovecraftian influence.

For the 50th anniversary, Puffin and BBC Worldwide has published a series of eleven eBook shorts based on each of the Eleven Doctors. Many popular British authors wrote these short stories on the Doctor – one for each, all appearing in 2013. Many of these names are well known among fantasy readers:

- First Doctor, William Hartnell (1963-1966) – Eoin Colfer, *A Big Hand For The Doctor* (Jan 23rd). Colfer writes the terribly popular *Artemis Fowl* books about a child mastermind battling fairies and more.
- Second Doctor, Patrick Troughton (1966-1969) - Michael Scott, *The Nameless City* (Feb 23rd). Scott is author of *The Secrets of the Immortal Nicholas Flamel* series.
- Third Doctor, Jon Pertwee (1970-1974) - Marcus Sedgwick, *The Spear of Destiny* (Mar 23rd). Author of children's books such as *The Dark Horse*.
- Fourth Doctor, Tom Baker (1974-1981) - Philip Reeve, *The Roots of Evil* (April 23rd). Author of the *Mortal Engines* series.
- Fifth Doctor, Peter Davison (1981-1984) - Patrick Ness, *Tip of the Tongue* (May 23rd). Author of *The Knife of Never Letting Go* (which won an enormous number of awards)
- Sixth Doctor, Colin Baker (1984-1986) - Richelle Mead, *Something Borrowed* (June 23rd). Author of *Vampire Academy*.
- Seventh Doctor, Sylvester McCoy (1987-1996) - Malorie Blackman, *The Ripple Effect* (July 23rd). The Children's Laureate of Britain for 2013 to 2015. Author of the *Noughts and Crosses* series.
- Eighth Doctor, Paul McGann (1996) - Alex Scarrow, *Spore* (Aug 23rd). Author of the *TimeRiders* series.

- Ninth Doctor, Christopher Eccleston (2005) - Charlie Higson, *The Beast of Babylon* (Sept 23rd). Author of the *Young Bond* series.
- Tenth Doctor, David Tennant (2005-2010) - Derek Landy, *The Mystery of the Haunted Cottage* (Oct 23rd). Author of the *Skulduggery Pleasant* novels.
- Eleventh Doctor, Matt Smith (2010-2013) - Neil Gaiman, *Nothing O'Clock* (Nov 21st). Neil Gaiman is the best-selling author of *Stardust, Neverwhere, The Graveyard Book* and *Coraline*. It's fitting he wrote the Eleventh Doctor as he also wrote two Eleventh Doctor episodes, *The Doctor's Wife* and *Nightmare in Silver*).

Most of these authors write *Harry Potter* competition from middle grade fantasy to slightly darker young adult works. In fact, Rowling was rumored for some time to be one of the chosen authors.

Classics

From 1975-1977, Doctor Who underwent a famously Gothic period, in which it retold many classics with a science fiction flavor: *The Mummy* ("Pyramids of Mars"), *Frankenstein* ("The Brain of Morbius"), *The Prisoner of Zenda* ("The Android Invasion") *Masque of the Red Death* ("The Masque of Mandragora") *The Hands of Orloc* ("The Hand of Fear"), *The Phantom of the Opera* ("The Deadly Assassin"), Jekyll and Hyde ("Planet of Evil"), Agatha Christie ("The Robots of Death"), Sherlock Holmes and Fu Manchu ("The Talons of Weng-Chiang"), The poem *Flannan Isle* by Wilfrid Wilson Gibson ("The Horror of Fang Rock"), *The Sirens of Titan* by Kurt Vonnegut and *Quatermass and the Pit* ("Image of the Fendahl") (Layton, *Humanism* 112; Newman 87).

> Often this took the form of remediating iconography and narrative tropes and techniques familiar from the Hammer films, which had in turn reinvented the 1930s Universal horror movies for a 1960s and 1970s audience. While "The Brain of Morbius" most obviously draws upon the Frankenstein myth – itself remediating aspects of the Greek myth of Prometheus – it also recasts Robert Louis Stevenson's *Strange Case of Dr Jekyll and Mr Hyde* in Doctor Who terms. The 1977 story "The Talons of Weng-Chiang" (written by Robert Holmes) draws heavily on various aspects of actual Victoriana as well as ideas of Victoriana. These range from Sherlock Holmes to Fu Manchu, the latter being a pulp character that while not strictly Victorian or even Edwardian is often erroneously associated with this era. In terms of "Pyramids," the influence of the Universal and Hammer versions of *The Mummy* and its sequels are obvious to see. (Harvey 28)

In the comics, novels, and audio dramas, the Doctors meet J.R.R. Tolkien, J.M. Barrie, Bram Stoker, Edgar Allen Poe, Oscar Wilde, Jane Austen, Jules Verne, George Bernard Shaw, George Orwell, and many others. In June 1816, Mary Shelley gets the idea for *Frankenstein* when she sees the Eighth Doctor apparently coming back to life, and even travels with him as a companion in *Mary's Story*. There's an actual alien invasion during Orson Welles' *War of the Worlds* radio drama.

The Doctor himself has startling similarities to heroes of the past—not as much action heroes (despite an occasional sword bout) but the more intellectual heroes—masterminds and tricksters from the classics:

> The same traits do turn up with great regularity in Nation's work. He did like a hero who eschews violence and relies on his own improvisations to escape dangerous situations. And a lot of it comes from the thrillers he read as a child. Heroes like Sherlock Holmes, the Scarlet Pimpernel, the Saint – these characters might occasionally resort to fisticuffs or even, in extremis, to a weapon, but mostly they depended on their wits. (Cawley, "Alwyn Turner on Terry Nation")

129

Sherlock Holmes

- ►◄ In "The Snowmen," the Eleventh Doctor presents himself as Sherlock Holmes in full costume. He parodies the famous character, exclaiming, "Now, shut up, don't tell me! I see from your collar stud you have an apple tree and a wife with a limp. Am I right?" This nods to Steven Moffat and Mark Gatiss's new show, *Sherlock*. In fact, a few bars of this show play to accompany his entrance.

- ►◄ Doyle also wrote *The Lost World*, about a hidden realm where dinosaurs still walk the earth, and one character manages to link these series together. When he meets the Silurian Vastra, Simeon tells her, "Doctor Doyle is almost certainly basing his fantastical tales on your own exploits. With a few choice alterations, of course. I doubt the readers of *The Strand* magazine would accept that the great detective is, in reality a woman." ("The Snowmen"). Watson can be logically extrapolated from a combination of Victorian Jenny and warrior-healer Strax.

- ►◄ The child Elliot Northover quotes Holmes, noting, "Once you eliminate the impossible, whatever remains, no matter how improbable, must be the truth." It seems more than coincidence that this takes place in the Silurian episode "The Hungry Earth."

- ►◄ In "Ghost Light," the second story in Season 26, the Seventh Doctor and Ace meet the explorer Redvers Fenn-Cooper, who mentions Doctor Doyle saw dinosaurs with him and thus wrote *The Lost World*.

- ►◄ Several novels including *Happy Endings, The Shape of Things,* and *All-Consuming Fire,* feature Holmes and Watson. The last of these is written as a typical Holmes adventure, with Watson as biographer. In the audio adventure *The Haunting of Thomas Brewster,* the Doctor dwells on Baker Street in Victorian London.

- ►◄ Tom Baker played Holmes in a 1982 television version of *The Hound of the Baskervilles.*

- The novel *Evolution* has Doyle dressing Holmes to imitate the Fourth Doctor's ensemble from "The Talons of Weng-Chiang," in a dizzyingly self-reflective moment, as the Doctor appeared to have been mimicking Holmes in the first place.
- In "The Name of the Doctor," the Doctor mentions a fond dream of retiring and taking up beekeeping – Sherlock Holmes' final fate.
- *Torchwood*'s "Small Worlds" references Doyle's connection with the Cottingley fairy photos.

Shakespeare
- "The Shakespeare Code" is filled with title references: the inn is called "The Tempest" and another inn, "The Elephant," appears in *Twelfth Night*. The Doctor uses the phrases "A Winter's Tale" and "Brave New World" (from *The Tempest*). The mad architect in 'Bedlam' is an allusion to Tom o' Bedlam from *King Lear,* who calls himself "Poor Peter" and speaks in third person in a direct allusion. They battle three witches, whom Shakespeare will presumably write about in *Macbeth*. He also plans to write *Hamlet* for his deceased son. He composes his most famous sonnet for Martha, his "dark lady." Ironically, Tennant went on to play Hamlet after his time on *Who*.
- The Doctor quotes *Hamlet* in several old episodes. Even Charles Dickens quotes Shakespeare.
- Likewise, the First Doctor and his companions use the Time-Space Visualiser to witness Shakespeare tell Francis Bacon a play about Hamlet would be foolish, and then later reconsider in "The Chase." In "Planet of Evil," "City of Death," and "Mark of the Rani," the Doctor mentions he's met Shakespeare before (only a slight contradiction with "The Shakespeare Code" as Shakespeare might not realize other Doctors were the same person or might have met them later in his life).

- Several novels and audio adventures feature meetings with the Bard.
- The Doctor tells a companion that he played the role of the Doctor in the first performance of *Macbeth* in 1609 before King James I in the novel *The Empire of Glass.*
- The novel *Managra* features Francis Pearson, a less-worthy contemporary of Shakespeare. His works include many parodies of Shakespeare titles: *Three Gentlemen of Venice on a Killing Spree*, *Edward II's Horrible End*, *The Adventures of Macbeth's Head*, and *Thirteenth Night.* He apparently burnt down the Globe theatre out of jealousy for Shakespeare on 29th June 1613 and disappeared. Many of his plays, such as *The Blood, Vampires: the Froth and the Frenzy* and *The Blood Countess of Transylvania* were inspired by The Countess Bathory, supposed by most to be a vampire. The novel references Shakespeare's *Henry VIII, Richard II, Macbeth, Twelfth Night, and Romeo and Juliet*, along with the Bible, Milton, Wordsworth, Sartre, *Frankenstein, Grimm's Fairytales, The Hitch-Hiker's Guide to the Galaxy, Don Juan, Childe Haroldes Pilgrimage, the Malleus Maleficarum,* the Zohar, Poe's "The Fall of the House of Usher," and Malory's *Morte d'Arthur.*
- Various *Doctor Who* audio plays reference Shakespeare in their titles:
  - *Full Fathom Five (The Tempest* I.ii)
  - *The Chimes of Midnight (Henry IV Part 2,* III.ii)
  - *He Jests at Scars... (Romeo and Juliet* II.ii)
- David Tennant has had a long Shakespeare career, as Hamlet in 2008 and then Benedick opposite Catherine Tate in a 2011 production of *Much Ado About Nothing.* In 2013-2014, he will play Richard II for the Royal Shakespeare Company.

132

More Classics

► The Fourth Doctor often quotes *Alice in Wonderland,* a concept that fits well with his eccentric nature. The Fifth Doctor declares (in something of a misquote) that like Alice, he tries to believe three impossible things before breakfast. ("The Five Doctors"). When companion Peri Brown is reading a copy of the book onboard the TARDIS, in the comic *Salad Days,* the Doctor's personal reality warp transports her into the world of the book. In the Eighth Doctor audio adventure *Zagreus,* the TARDIS gives him hints out of the book and even manifests a Cheshire Cat to guide him. The alien Zagreus in turn manifests a Jabberwocky.

► In the Eighth Doctor Big Finish audio adventure, *Nevermore,* there's a prison world inspired by Poe, with robotic raven jailors and a mist called the Red Death.

► H.G. Wells was inspired to write his beloved books and also coined the phrase "science fiction" after meeting the Sixth Doctor ("Timelash"). In the comic *The Time Machination*, the Tenth Doctor meets HG Wells (who had previously met the Sixth Doctor). Wells is captured by Torchwood, and has an adventure with them. Meanwhile, the Tenth Doctor wears the deerstalker and plaid Sherlock Holmes getup, only to leave seconds before the Fourth Doctor's arrival in the same outfit...he's traveling with Leela in "The Talons of Wang Chiang." "How many of you are there, Doctor?" Wells asks.

► "Abandon hope all ye who enter here," quoted in "The Mind of Evil," is from Dante's *Inferno.*

► Roberts and Davies stuffed as many of Agatha Christie's works as they could reference into "The Unicorn and the Wasp." Titles used in the show include: *The Murder of Roger Ackroyd; Why Didn't They Ask Evans; The Body in the Library; The Secret Adversary; N or M?; Nemesis; Cat Among the Pigeons; Dead Man's Folly; They Do It With Mirrors; Appointment with Death; Cards on the Table; Sparkling*

Cyanide; Endless Night; Crooked House; The Moving Finger; Taken at the Flood; Death Comes as the End; Murder on the Orient Express and *The Murder at the Vicarage*. The murder mystery mirrors several of Christie's novels: the jewel theft storyline parallels *The Secret of Chimneys*; *Crooked House* features secrets within an aristocratic society, Miss Chandrakala's death is from *And Then There Were None*; and the Colonel's faking being disabled is seen in *The Pale Horse*. They finally all meet in "The accusing parlor." Christie's grandson, Mathew Prichard, represented her estate and attended the episode's readthrough. He gave his enthusiastic approval to Doctor Who's portrayal of his grandmother.

- Simon Callow, who portrayed Dickens, is a strong scholar and recreator of Dickens's life. Callow only agreed to the part after he discovered the centrality and respect Dickens received in the episode. In "The Unquiet Dead," he's touring with *A Christmas Carol*. Dickens plans to use the Gelth in his novel *The Mystery of Edwin Drood*, which famously was never finished.
- Susie Costello of *Torchwood* links her lockdown code to *The Complete Works of Emily Dickinson*.
- The comic *The Man in the Ion Mask* with an imprisoned Master references the similarly-named Dumas novel.
- "All right, Quasimodo, time to do your thing," Clyde says, ringing the chapel bell in SJA: "Eye of the Gorgon" part 2.
- "The Empty Child" and "The Doctor Dances" involve Jack's relationship with Algy, a likely reference to the heroes of *The Importance of Being Earnest*. The tale of a band of orphans stealing from the wealthier class (and led by a girl named Nancy!) seems to be an *Oliver Twist* homage.
- Dr. Renfrew from "Day of the Moon" seems to echo Renfield, the brainwashed sycophant in *Dracula*.
- For the episode "A Christmas Carol," producer Piers Wenger notes, "It kind of riffs on the Dickens story.

There's no one called Scrooge in it and it's not set on Earth, but there are familiar archetypes from that story within it that will please fans of Dickens's original" (Soghomonian). As the Doctor and companions play the three ghosts and blend time travel and Dickens, an echo of the original story remains.

- In "The Curse of the Black Spot," the "black spot" itself comes from *Treasure Island*...though it also appeared in the *Pirates of the Caribbean* franchise. The latter, like the episode, deals with a boy discovering his father is a pirate.
- The title of "Tooth and Claw" is an allusion to the line "Nature, red in tooth and claw" from Tennyson's *In Memoriam A.H.H.* The poem was a favorite of Queen Victoria's. The Doctor also references the Scottish ballad Walter Lesly ("I've been chasin' this – this wee naked child over hill and over dale,") and Robert Burns's poem *To a Mouse* ("Isn't that right, ye tim'rous beastie?") to explain his and Rose's strange attire.
- The family in "The Fires Of Pompeii" is inspired by the first book of the Cambridge Latin Course from 1970, focusing on the banker named Lucius Caecilius Iucundus, his wife Metella, and his son Quintus.
- "Daleks in Manhattan" features the character Tallulah, based on Jodie Foster's Tallulah in *Bugsy Malone* or the actress Talullah Bankhead. It combines themes and tropes from the horror stories *The Island of Doctor Moreau*, *Frankenstein* and *The Phantom of the Opera*.
- Amy Pond spends "The Beast Below" in her nightie, a reference to childish adventures like *Hitchhiker's Guide* or *Peter Pan*. Moffat wanted to create a childlike relationship between the Eleventh Doctor and Amy, like the one of Peter Pan and Wendy (Audio Commentary). On their first meeting, as the Doctor insists he loves a food then spits it out, he seems to be evoking Tigger, something critics note as they insist "Moffat [is]

deliberately casting them as a version of Tigger and Winnie-the-Pooh" (Hoskin 133).

> The basis of the relationship between the Doctor and the companion really is a magic man from space and a child... It's not boyfriend and girlfriend, it's not husband and wife, God knows, it's actually a magic man from space who can take you away, means you never have to go back to school, and a child. And that remains their relationship even when they're growed up a bit. - Steven Moffat (qtd. in Hoskin 133)

►◄ Clara's job as a governess whose two charges are haunted by the ghost of her predecessor is taken from the Victorian classic *The Turn of the Screw*.

Religion

The show's take on religion varies through the series. Certainly, Arthur C. Clarke's "Third Law" applies. It states "Any sufficiently advanced technology is indistinguishable from magic," and many cultures are seen worshipping sophisticated aliens, or believing them supernatural creatures. The Tenth Doctor mentions that he doesn't believe in any specific god, but has met a number of beings who claimed to be gods. He also mentions a universe of religions, including "The Archiphets, Orkology, Christianity, Pash Pash, New Judaism, San Klah, Church of the Tin Vagabond" ("The Satan Pit"). The greatest apotheosis is "The Last of the Time Lords." As Ten swells with the power of humanity's belief, he's filled with golden light and literally becomes a god. This episode "replays long standing myths and gives them a religious character" (Layton, *Humanism* 133). The Ninth Doctor notes, "Don't worship me. I'd make a very bad god" ("Boom Town"), but the Tenth Doctor requires worship to save the earth.

The Doctor was apparently present at Jesus Christ's birth (at which he took that last room at the inn) ("Voyage of the Damned") and the first Easter ("Planet of the Dead"), and was also involved in the Crusades and the Catholic-Protestant altercation known as the Massacre of Saint Bartholomew's Day.

The Ninth Doctor hints that he's Santa Claus and he had delivered a red bicycle to a twelve-year-old Rose Tyler ("The Doctor Dances"). It's also notable that young Amelia Pond prays to Santa and the Eleventh Doctor arrives. The latter also jumps down a chimney in "A Christmas Carol," but adds that the "big fat guy" will be down later. The First and Second Doctors meet Santa in comics and prose.

Angels

The Host from "Voyage of the Damned" continue the motif of angels seen in the Weeping Angels and also the Master's "Archangel Network." The Host are shown as a neutral force – horrific when programmed to kill, but then persuaded to accept the Doctor as their new authority. This may be a subtle comment on religion's power to murder and terrorize or redeem, depending who wields it. The weeping angels are a force of horror, made worse by their nonthreatening appearance.

Angels as glowing, beatific beings of light are seen as Solonians in their "evolved form" ("The Mutants") or Light in "Ghost Light." Gwyneth believed that the Gelth were angels on "The Unquiet Dead." Peter Dalton, on the edge of death, believed that the otherworldly Trickster was an angel ("The Wedding of Sarah Jane Smith"). Both of course are being exploited by aliens. In his Miracle Day speech, Oswald Danes claims that humanity had evolved into angels, but he clearly has a skewed view of morality ("The Categories of Life").

The people of medieval Europe have no concept of aliens, only guiding angels. As such, both the Doctor himself and other aliens and time travelers are often considered angels, particularly in comics and novels. Thus Madame de Pompadour calls the Tenth Doctor "her lonely angel" ("The Girl in the Fireplace"). Rani Chandra returns to the future after befriending Jane Grey, and Jane believes Rani to have been an angel (SJA: "Lost in Time"). In the novel *The Empire of Glass,* Cardinal Robert

Bellarmine mediates the Armageddon Convention in 1609, believing that he's settling a war between angels. In 1669, Father Chadwick Vita thinks that the alien Healer is an angel in the comic, *Black Death White Life.*

Other References
- The Master masquerades as a Christian priest in "The Dæmons," while another Time Lord is known as the Meddling Monk.
- The ghosts of "Army of Ghosts" or "The Unquiet Dead" are actually an alien hoax to gain power over humanity. "Hide" is not a ghostly encounter, but another tale entirely.
- Several arks that carry humanity from a dying earth seem to reference to Biblical story of Noah (particularly "The Ark" and "The Ark in Space." The Fourth Doctor mentions this concept directly in "Full Circle," while the leader of Nerva Beacon on "The Ark in Space" is nicknamed Noah.
- The Doctor is poisoned with a toxin derived from the Judas Tree in "Let's Kill Hitler." Melody administers the toxin by betraying him, casting the Doctor as Christ.
- "Guests are reminded that Platform 1 forbids the use of weapons, teleportation, and religion." ("The End of the World")
- The Bishop and army of Clerics of the future aid the Eleventh Doctor and River in the 51st century crash of the Byzantium. The former comments, "It's the fifty first Century. The Church has moved on" ("Time of the Angels"). In the 52nd century, the Silence, the Church and the Order of the Headless are allied to kill the Doctor before he can ask the Ultimate Question ("The Impossible Astronaut, "A Good Man Goes to War, "The Wedding of River Song").
- K'anpo Rimpoche, abbot of a Buddhist meditation center in England, helped the Third Doctor regenerate in "Planet of the Spiders."

- Marco Polo and Barbara Wright visit the Cave of the Thousand Buddhas in "Marco Polo." A Buddhist Monastery, the Dat-Sen in Tibet appears in "The Abominable Snowmen."
- While "Gridlock" is a bleak comment on modern traffic, the people at the end witness the heavens opening and they sing the hymn "Abide with Me." While trapped on the gloomy Motorway, they sing "The Old Rugged Cross."
- "Planet of the Dead" doesn't bring up its Easter Special timing, only a quick mention of "robot bunnies carrying baskets full of deadly egg bombs."
- Lazarus is the biblical character Jesus raised from the dead. When he revives in "The Lazarus Experiment," the Doctor comments that he should have expected it.
- When the Doctor and Martha first enter Hooverville in "Daleks in Manhattan," two men are arguing about bread. Solomon divides the loaf, a reference to the Judgment of Solomon.

TV
EastEnders
- The Doctor's line "This'll be the best Christmas Walford has ever had" in "The Impossible Planet" is a line from *EastEnders*,
- The exterior of the Queen Vic pub from the BBC soap *EastEnders* can be seen in the Starship UK's shopping area ("The Beast Below").
- Pooky Quesnel, who plays the starliner captain in "A Christmas Carol" is most famous for portraying devoted Doctor Who fan Bradley Branning's mother in *EastEnders*.
- "The Doctor's back there in Eastenders-land and we're stuck here in the past!" ("Night Terrors")
- *Dimensions in Time,* the 30th anniversary *Doctor Who* special, was a crossover with EastEnders.

More TV

> Some episodes, such as "The Web of Fear," have
> sensibilities similar to those of *The Twilight Zone*,
> while others, like "The Aztecs," seem more like a
> lost episode of *Masterpiece Theatre*. Other creative
> influences include steampunk, the fantasy films of
> Jim Henson, the comedy of Monty Python and
> Douglas Adams, the science fiction of Ursula K.
> LeGuin, and the postmodern cynicism and hip
> sensibilities of *Buffy the Vampire Slayer*. Because
> the series was on the air for so many decades,
> there are those who love different eras of the show.
> (DiPaolo 966)

- The craze for Steampunk is reflected in a few episodes: Paul McGann in Victorian Dress with a newly revised TARDIS in the film, the kid-powered giant Cyberking of "The Next Doctor," alien bounty hunters in the town of Mercy, the clockwork robots in France.
- The Doctor's befuddled near-asexuality is often played for laughs or a comment on how alien he is. This asexual genius archetype shows up in several series: many Sherlock Holmes characters, from the original to the reboot of *Sherlock*. Spock, Sheldon, Mr. Data, *Voyager*'s Doctor. One critic notes:

> An adult character not remotely concerned with all
> that might actually be refreshing - not as a comedic
> naïf foil for others (Sheldon in The Big Bang
> Theory), but as someone who is fun and funny and
> smart and clever and still not obsessed with, nor
> actively pursuing, sex. The Doctor is that character.
> Right now. That doesn't mean he's not sexy. Mr
> Spock, another cultural icon, was sexy without
> being remotely interested in sex (most of the time).
> In the world of fiction and fantasy, there is nothing
> sexier than a guy who isn't interested. (Hale, Kindle
> Locations 5269-5274)

- The Martha Jones episode "42" plays out in real time, much like the show of its inverted title, *24*. Of course, 42 also references *Hitchhiker's Guide* and longtime *Who* writer Douglas Adams, and also nods to the number of minutes in a *New Who* episode. It contains a number of trivia questions Martha must solve, in a subtle gameshow reference.
- "The Fires of Pompeii" was filmed in the same studio that does *Rome*, on location in Italy – the first time that an ongoing *Doctor Who* series had taken its principal cast abroad since "The Two Doctors" was recorded in Seville in 1985.
- The season arc is a relatively recent phenomenon: "[*Doctor Who*'s] strength, however, is not its one-off stories but its longer arcs, a structural breakthrough of *The X-Files*, which modeled the notion that episodic TV could be woven together with powerful, season-long themes, inspiring the more complex breed of modern shows, both sci-fi and regular-fi." (Nussbaum 127)
- In "Bad Wolf," Anne Robinson was invited to voice the Anne Droid, though the producers expected she would decline. To their delight, she accepted the job ("The World of Who"). While playing on the reality TV show, the Davinadroid voice asks the Doctor not to swear, echoing Davina McCall's requests in the actual *Big Brother* program. The *Big Brother UK TV Theme* plays during the show. Further, the Doctor's final line is "I'm coming to get you," the traditional line said the contestants evicted from the house in the UK. Lynda mentions many popular UK reality shows: *The Weakest Link, Call My Bluff, Countdown, Ground Force, Wipeout* and *Stars in Their Eyes*.
- In "The Age of Steel," Pete calls the Preachers "Scooby-Doo and his gang" driving the Mystery Machine.
- *Torchwood* has many parallels with *Angel*. They're led by a troubled warrior who's ancient and invincible in a striking coat and with their team of five (brainy girl

scientist, woman who represents the team's heart and wants a normal life, etc.). They battle the paranormal with darker, more adult themes than their family-friendly spinoff.

- *Torchwood,* as a secret organization protecting earth from alien life, follows the tropes of *Men in Black, Warehouse 13, X-Files, Sanctuary,* etc.
- In the late 1980s, *Doctor Who* aired opposite *Coronation Street,* possibly a factor in the show's decline and cancellation in 1989. In the short story "Christmas Special" the Sixth Doctor dreams his adventures are on television opposite this show, in a terribly metafictional moment. *Coronation Street* occasionally references *Doctor Who* in turn, with Simon Barlow as an eager fan.
- The "Royal Hope Hospital" name from "Smith and Jones" was reused in the pilot episode of *Law & Order: UK,* starring Freema Agyeman, written by former *Doctor Who* writer Chris Chibnall.
- In "The Snowmen," Dr. Simeon announces repeatedly that "Winter is Coming," a *Game of Thrones* catchphrase.
- Toby Whithouse wrote the episode "The God Complex" as well as creating *Being Human* (Dan Martin). Both feature attempts to combine the supernatural with everyday reality.
- When the Doctor arrives in the lift in "Evolution of the Daleks," he says "First Floor, Perfumery," echoing the BBC sitcom *Are You Being Served?* (There the line is "Ground Floor, Perfumery," but in the US the Ground Floor is called the "First Floor.")
- "Smith and Jones" features an alien who sucks blood with a bendy straw, also seen in *The Fairly Oddparents* and an episode of *Red Dwarf.*
- New New York may be a reference to the similar city in *Futurama.*
- *The Simpsons* appears in the Ood who can shout "D'oh!" in "Planet of the Ood" (dubbed a "comedy classic option") and the Tenth Doctor's complaint of "Worst.

Rescue. Ever!" in "The End of Time," echoing Comic Book Guy's catchphrase.

Movie

- ●▪ Rory watches the Doctor goof off within *The Flying Deuces* in "The Impossible Astronaut."
- ●▪ "Voyage of the Damned" evokes *The Poseidon Adventure*, and is certainly modeled after classic disaster movies.
- ●▪ "Voyage of the Damned" also contains many shout outs to *Doctor Who* and *Blake's 7* script editor Chris Boucher: The Hosts resemble the killer robots in Boucher's Fourth Doctor story "The Robots of Death." The damaged Host repeating "Kill...kill," the Host's hand stuck in the door, and the secret room full of Hosts on stretchers also appear in that story. The teleport bracelets are from *Blake's 7*, and the Angels' "Information" catchphrase is from Zen, *Blake's 7*'s *Liberator* computer.
- ●▪ Davies described "Planet of the Dead" as "a great big adventure, a little bit *Indiana Jones*, a little bit *Flight of the Phoenix*, a little bit *Pitch Black*" (Colville). In fact, "Planet of the Dead" combines many films, with half-man, half-insect aliens partly inspired by *The Fly*. Davies invented a cat burglar inspired by DC Comics' Black Canary who is introduced in a *Mission: Impossible* sequence. Davies also pictured the Doctor and cat burglar having a relationship like that of Cary Grant and Audrey Hepburn in the 1963 thriller *Charade*.
- ●▪ Davies' inspiration for "Turn Left" was the 1998 Gwyneth Paltrow film *Sliding Doors,* which explores two sets of consequences of whether or not a woman catches a train. He originally intended to use this device to introduce the new Series Four companion, before Donna Noble returned instead. "Turn Left" also has a decidedly *It's a Wonderful Life* motif, as Donna sees what the universe would be like without her as companion.

- "Bad Wolf" is inspired by *Minority Report*, with a pale, androgynous Controller.
- In "Day of the Moon," the post-hypnotic suggestion echoes *The Manchurian Candidate,* while transmitters implanted in their hands suggest *A Beautiful Mind.* The short-term memory loss and notes on the skin hint at *Momento.* The creepy orphanage triggers thoughts of *The Shining.* The ending in the alleyway is shot like the beginning of *The Terminator* – both are tales of an assassin from the future, come to change the past.
- The Men in Black on a mission to cover up alien attacks are a popular element of UFO culture and have featured in several series, especially the Will Smith and Tommy Lee Jones films. The *Doctor Who* serial *Dreamland* and *The Sarah Jane Adventures* feature these mysterious figures, in this case, long-lived androids.
- The title "The Shakespeare Code" echoes *The Da Vinci Code*, especially with its theme of a deep mystical code innocuously hidden in the classics.
- "Midnight" is eerily different from most *Doctor Who* episodes – the Doctor never solves the mystery or settles things with the unknown alien, but must leave the encounter shaking with horror, much like the audience.

> The episode is similar in message and tone to the Stephen King story *The Mist* and is one of the few Davies episodes embraced by the die-hard fans of the original Doctor Who series who tend to dislike Davies' work. Nevertheless, "Midnight" seems like a nod in the direction of the traditionalist fans – an old-school Gothic Doctor Who adventure. (DiPaolo 975)

- The climax of "The Age of Steel," as Mickey takes the name Ricky and stays to fight the good fight, encouraging his true love to leave with another man, is very *Casablanca.* Mickey even says he'll free Paris.

- The werewolf transformation in "Tooth and Claw" echoes *Thriller* and *An American Werewolf in London*.
- The hidden room under Stonehenge, with cobwebs and flaming torches echoes *Indiana Jones* – in fact, the *Doctor Who Confidential* showed how the director used a playback of *Raiders of the Lost Ark* soundtrack during filming. River Song, of course, is an action-packed archeologist who shoots everything in sight.
- In "The Wedding of River Song," the Doctor thinks that Gantok has mentioned "rats" instead of "traps," then he falls into a pit of skulls. This is another *Indiana Jones* nod, along with the spooky tunnel through which they walk.
- In the television movie, the Master forces the Eighth Doctor's eyes open with a frightening device in *Clockwork Orange* style. The Doctor regenerates and stumbles from the morgue in scenes alternating with Frankenstein's Monster coming to life in the black-and-white movie the morgue attendant is watching.
- News entries with changing text and flaming tire trails in "The Waters of Mars" echo *Back to the Future*. There are other ties as people face being erased from history when the timelines change. Producer Piers Wenger gushes:

> I love that movie! That's one of the movies that I absolutely loved when I grew up. Michael J. Fox was incredibly cool! And I think even Steven [Moffat]'s writing is preoccupied with individual timelines and what happens when timelines cross and how if you go back and change the past the impact it will on your future. That is one of the great elements of *Doctor Who* and I guess of any show that is concerned with time travel. (Soghomonian)

- In "The Waters of Mars," a character is infected by a single drop falling onto his eye, rather like *28 Days Later*.
- The joke in "Dalek" of an alien hairdryer being mistaken for a weapon is from *Buck Rogers in the 25th Century*.

- Tony Curran (Van Gogh) once played an Invisible Man in *The League of Extraordinary Gentlemen*. His episode features an invisible monster.
- In "The Fires of Pompeii," the Doctor introduces himself with "I am... Spartacus." Donna adds, "And so am I."
- The "Night Terrors" scene in which the Doctor and Alex gets sucked into the child's cupboard echoes a similar scene from *Poltergeist*. Being yanked into a doll's house is very *Tales of the Darkside*.
- In "The Vampires of Venice," the Doctor references *The Wicker Man* and the girls' look is a deliberate homage to the Hammer Horror era. Rory's use of crossed candlesticks as a cross also happens in the 1958 *Dracula*. Isabella's demise echoes the very first death in *Jaws* – they even play the theme during that scene in the *Doctor Who Confidential*.
- The Third Doctor's fast cars and spy adventures for UNIT were deliberately modeled after James Bond. Matt Smith adds, "I was talking to Steven Moffat about it the other day and we were saying when I started there was sort of uproar at my age and everything, and then when Daniel Craig started there was uproar, how can Daniel Craig be James Bond? And now look at him, we're on the cusp of possibly the greatest James Bond movie ever" (Weintraub). Ianto introduces himself to Jack as "Jones. Ianto Jones." In the novels, he enjoys *James Bond* marathons. In "The Lazarus Experiment," Martha says the Doctor in a tux looks like James Bond (he appears flattered). The commentary track mentions the Doctor's loosening of his bow-tie as a "Daniel Craig moment."
- River's relationship with the Doctor, a time traveler who meets her in the wrong order, seems to echo *The Time Traveler's Wife,* as does "The Girl in the Fireplace."
- The Eleventh Doctor gives River the codename "Mrs. Robinson," referencing an older seductress of a younger

man in *The Graduate*. She's not amused ("The Impossible Astronaut").

➤ In "Let's Kill Hitler," a robot that appears human and mimics appearances travels to the past to assassinate a future leader, followed by Melody Pond saying, "Take off your clothes." It's very *Terminator*.

➤ The running gag of the Doctor replacing enemies' guns with bananas is a reference to Buster Keaton's similar gag in *The High Sign*.

➤ In "The Christmas Invasion," the Doctor entreats the Sycorax to leave the humans alone because from the day they arrive on the planet, and blinking, step into the sun, there is more to be seen than can ever be seen... then he stops himself and says, "Wait, that's *The Lion King*."

➤ The sequence in "The Time of Angels" with the Weeping Angel slowly emerging from the television screen is a possible reference to *The Ring*.

➤ The Doctor tells Shakespeare that Martha's from Freedonia, a country name best known from the Marx Brothers movie *Duck Soup*.

➤ The Doctor explains time travel using *Back to the Future* (the movie, not the novelization) in "The Shakespeare Code."

> DOCTOR: Oh, how to explain the mechanics of the infinite temporal flux? I know. *Back to the Future*. It's like *Back to the Future*.
> MARTHA: The film?
> DOCTOR: No, the novelization. Yes, the film. Marty McFly goes back and changes history.
> MARTHA: And he starts fading away. Oh my God, am I going to fade?
> DOCTOR: You and the entire future of the human race. It ends right now in 1599 if we don't stop it. ("The Shakespeare Code")

➤ In "The Snowmen," Clara uses the Mary Poppins line "The position has been filled," then whisks into the sky with the aid of an umbrella. As he takes on a role as babysitter, the Doctor wonders whether twelve-and-a-half-year-old Kazran Sardick had seen Mary Poppins, but stops himself, adding that the analogy would have been "rubbish" ("A Christmas Carol"). In the novel *Magic of the Angels,* the Eleventh Doctor gathers magician props and stuffs them in a carpet bag that's bigger on the inside than the outside, saying he's glad he got it back from Mary Poppins.

- Referencing *Dr. Strangelove,* Jack Harkness rides the bomb in "The Doctor Dances."
- In Erasmus' lab, Clyde comments: "This is Hogwarts Tim Burton style! It's... Harry Potter has a close shave off Sweeney Todd." Later, Rani remarks: "This is worse than *The Sixth Sense*" (SJA: "The Eternity Trap").
- The Tenth Doctor gets in a "Who you gonna call" while investigating the Ghost Shifts, and the music mimics the movie theme ("Army of Ghosts"). Clara Oswald calls herself and the Doctor "ghostbusters" during introductions to Emma Grayling and Alec Palmer in "Hide." In "The Eternity Trap," Clyde wisecracks, "I ain't afraid of no ghost." Later, he says "We've come to bust you," and Rani adds, "I'd feel a whole lot better if I was wearing a Ghostbusters Proton Pack right now."
- "The Rebel Flesh" has many movie echoes. The Gangers are like the Replicants of *Blade Runner,* with shapeshifting visages reminiscent of *Star Trek*'s Odo, Voldemort, *The Thing,* and many other characters. Ganger Jennifer slowly takes on definition in a similar style to *Invasion of the Body Snatchers.* The harnessed workers controlling clones of themselves echoes *Avatar.*
- The director of *E.T.,* Steven Spielberg, once held the theatrical film rights to *Doctor Who,* leading to the Paul McGann television movie. His own movie gets a few particular *Doctor Who* references. When a spaceship lands in the Thames, some people hold up an "'Ello ET banner." In "Smith and Jones," the Tenth Doctor

wonders if the hospital has an "ET Department." When Androvax possesses a woman's body, Clyde tries to comfort the woman's daughter by suggesting Androvax only wants to "phone home" (SJA: "Prisoner of the Judoon"). He also suggests "E.T. the ASBO" must have stolen his bike in "Mona Lisa's Revenge."

- In "The Temptation of Sarah Jane Smith," Sarah Jane and Luke travel back in time and introduce themselves as Victoria and David Beckham.
- "Dinosaurs on a Spaceship" shows the game hunter Riddell holding off raptors with a tranquilizer gun while drinking from a hip flask, in a *Jurassic Park* echo.
- In "The Big Bang," the Doctor claims Amy is only mostly dead, a *Princess Bride* reference.

Comics

- The endless traffic jam in a dystopian future in "Gridlock" references Mega-City One in *Judge Dredd*. Both stories even have a man with a bowler hat.
- The Valiant, in "The Sound of Drums" is likely a homage to *Cloudbase*.
- Astrid Peth was inspired by Halo Jones, the science-fiction heroine of *2000 AD*.
- Rose's costume in "The Empty Child" nods to Jenny Spark's iconic one from *The Authority* comic books.
- Clyde notes, "I tell you, my Clydey-sense is tingling" (SJA: "The Temptation of Sarah Jane Smith" part 1).
- "The Lazarus Experiment" with its "mad scientist" imitates famous superhero villains, and indeed, the writer and producers brainstormed with Marvel superhero comic books, such as Spider-Man foes Doctor Octopus and the Green Goblin.

Myth and Folklore

● Werewolves and vampires appear in new episodes and old. "The Vampire Mutations," a Dracula retelling planned for the esventies' Gothic trend, was cancelled for fear of detracting from the similarly-timed BBC's *Count Dracula*. The episode was rewritten as 1980's "State of Decay" (Newman 87). In this, vampires are alien parasites--K-9 notes that 19 different planets have tales of vampires. These vampires, once fought by the Time Lords and now dwelling in e-space, have pale skin and fangs. When their king is destroyed, they crumble into death. Likewise, "The Claws of Axos" was originally called "Vampire from Space" (Newman 87).

● The Doctor encounters alien werewolves in "The Greatest Show in the Galaxy," the Eighth Doctor novel *Kursaal* and "Tooth and Claw." In the novel *Wolfsbane,* Harry Sullivan dies, and the Doctor and Sarah must try to solve the mystery. To recover their friend, they must deal with a heartbroken werewolf, a mysterious dryad, an Arthurian knight, and all manner of adventures. *Loups-Garoux* also features traditional werewolves in 2080 Rio de Jainero in a Big Finish Audio Adventure featuring the Fifth Doctor and Turlough.

● The Dæmons of the episode of that name reportedly inspired the horned gods and demons of earth, including Pan and Khnum. The Master, garbed in ceremonial robes and surrounded by thirteen acolytes, starts a summoning ritual in the church catacombs. He chants until the daemon Azal appears. However, while Azal looks supernatural, he is a mortal alien.

● The Doctor's fate of being sealed in the Pandorica (and his warning the world will be destroyed as a result) is quite similar to Merlin's famous fate, sealed in an impenetrable cave, which leads to the fall of Camelot. The Seventh Doctor is informed that he will become Merlin someday – hardly a shock as they're similar characters. One critic notes, "The Doctor has always been Merlin, symbolically speaking, so it's good to know that he finally gets to play the part" (Cornell, Topping, and Day, 340).

🎀 The Number of the Beast, 666, has appeared in multiple episodes, including "The Christmas Invasion," "The Impossible Planet," "Doomsday," "Voyage of the Damned," "Midnight," "The Stolen Earth," "Planet of the Dead," "The Doctor's Daughter," and TW: "They Keep Killing Suzie." Abaddon is the "son of the Beast" on *Torchwood's* "End of Days."

> DOCTOR: ...you'd need a power source with an inverted self-extrapolating reflex of six to the power of six every six seconds.
> ROSE: That's a lot of sixes. ("The Impossible Planet")

For "The Impossible Planet"/"The Satan Pit," the story's two episodes were even broadcast on either side of the week of 6 June 2006 (06/06/06).

🎀 "Chronos" of "The Time Monster" inspired the Greek god, but is revealed to be little more than a beast.

🎀 Commander Millington in "The Curse of Fenric" is obsessed with Norse mythology and preparing for Ragnarok, the end of the world. He tries to summon Fenric, based on the mythic wolf Fenrir. The Seventh Doctor calls Fenric an "evil from the dawn of time."

🎀 The extraterrestrial Osirians were most of the Egyptian gods, as revealed in "Pyramids of Mars." This becomes one of many stories "that place godlike beings in the far ancient times of the universe when it first began and that assert that modern people can do without such beings" (Layton, *Humanism* 136).

🎀 On *The Sarah Jane Adventures*, the Gorgons control a sect of Christian nuns ("Eye of the Gorgon"). They are parasites that require human hosts, and can indeed turn humans to stone. According to the episode, three Gorgons came to Earth around 1000 BC via a talisman.

151

One Gorgon was slain by a Greek hero (presumably Perseus), another by an archeologist couple in 1959, and the other by Maria Jackson and her friends in 2007. The First Doctor defeats a different type of Gorgon in the comic *The Gaze of the Gorgon*. In both encounters, mirrors and blindfolds prove the key.

- The Fourth Doctor and Romana encounter the Cailleach, Druidic goddess of war and magic, and nearly become sacrifices in "The Stones of Blood." Vivien Fay, a local village woman, is actually the dark goddess in disguise (her last name serves as a hint) and also the target of alien bounty hunters the Megara, whose callous literal-mindedness seems a precursor to the Judoon.

- In 16th century Europe, Susan tosses a part of a Liciax ship out onto earth, thinking it was a meteorite. However, it ends up in Prague where it's made into a golem and creates the famous legend, according to the short story "Life from Lifelessness."

- The Loch Ness Monster is a shadowy figure possibly inspired by the alien Skarasen, brought to Earth by the Zygons ("Terror of the Zygons") Another possible Loch Ness Monster is the Borad from the planet Karfel ("Timelash").

- The Eleventh Doctor calls the alien doctor who stalks the *Fancy* a mermaid or a siren. ("The Curse of the Black Spot"). The captain and crew assume the same, as it marks them with a black spot and carries them away if it senses they're wounded in any way.

- There are three Atlantis cities on the television show, in "The Underwater Menace," "The Dæmons," and "The Time Monster," but none of them correspond logically with one another.

- Several Minotaurs appear in the series: the Second Doctor and Zoe encounter one in the Land of Fiction and the Eighth Doctor encounters a similarly fictional Minotaur in the audio adventure *Caerdroia*. The Third

Doctor meets one in Atlantis--the creature once wished for the strength of a bull and got its wish, as the guardian of the Crystal of Kronos. At last, the Doctor defeats it. ("The Time Monster"). The Fourth Doctor also claims to have given the hero Theseus the ball of string that he used to find his way to the Minotaur in its labyrinth ("The Creature from the Pit"). Alien Minotaurs include the Nimons, the related species of "The God Complex," and the Tauride and Taureau races from various comics

- Professor Travers goes on a Yeti-seeking expedition in 1935 in "The Abominable Snowmen." However, the reported Yetis are actually robotic, created by the Great Intelligence. In the comic sequel *Yonder...the Yeti,* the Dali Lama blows a great horn and summons real Yeti to fight against their robotic counterparts. A Yeti (either live or robotic) is present in the Death Zone on Gallifrey for "The Five Doctors."

- The Fourth Doctor comments that "The living are just the dead on vacation" and tells Romana one could identify a genuine zombie by the fact that their skin was cold to the touch ("Destiny of the Daleks"). Rose Tyler calls the Gelth and people with the Empty Child virus zombies, which of course isn't literally true.

- Unicorns appear in the Land of Fiction, and according to *The Brilliant Book 2012,* in the alternate world of "The Wedding of River Song," unicorns are a pest in London, alongside Cyclopes and Satyrs (in the "normal world," no unicorns have been seen).

- In the comic, *Space Vikings!* the Tenth Doctor visits the Halls of Asgard and meets gods of Norse myth like Odin and the Valkyries.

- In the novel *Managra,* the Fourth Doctor and Sarah Jane visit Europa, a fantastical theme park planet filled with historical and mythic characters. They meet Lord Byron, several Casanovas, Mary Shelley, and Faust. Thanks to psychotronic engineering, the forests are filled with

153

ghosts, ghouls, werewolves, vampires and other creatures. "Europa is infested by ghosts, vampires, werewolves, ghouls and other grotesques spawned from old European folklore. I think we're in a spot of bother, Sarah Jane."

>< Katarina, a brief First Doctor companion from the Trojan War, travels through Hades and meets Cerberus and Charon in the short story "Katarina in the Underworld"

>< When Owen Harper is resurrected with the gauntlet on *Torchwood's* "Dead Man Walking," Death possesses him and tries to make him kill thirteen people so death can reenter the world. While possessing him, it repeats, "I shall walk the earth and my hunger will know no bounds" in a strange language. Eventually, Owen fights Death off before the murders are complete.

>< The Night Travelers, corresponding to various mysterious figures from folklore, are a travelling circus group that "come from out of the rain" on *Torchwood*.

>< The audio adventure *Frostfire* features a telepathic phoenix – a bird made of living flame known as a Cinder. They are actually energy-draining creatures from another dimension.

>< Fairies appear in Torchwood's "Small Worlds" with two forms: tiny beings of light and a human-sized, more monstrous form. They have lived on earth since the beginning of time, and thus aren't aliens. Fairies control the elements and can produce localized storms. They can time-travel and become invisible. Most importantly, they like children and will happily steal them away. Jack Harkness explains:

> They're part of us, part of our world, yet we know nothing about them. So we pretend to know what they look like. We see them as happy. We imagine they have tiny little wings and are bathed in moonlight...a touch of myth, a touch of the spirit world, a touch of reality, all jumbled together. Old

154

> moments and memories that are frozen in amongst it. Like debris spinning around a ringed planet - tossing, turning, whirling. Then backwards and forwards through time. If that's them we have to find them...before all hell breaks loose.

- The classic episode "Underworld" retells Jason and the Argonauts – Jackson quests for the golden cylindrical race banks rather than Jason questing for the golden fleece.
- The Barbary Terror, also called the White Terror, is a supernatural being which steals the souls of lost sailors at sea. Captain Benjamin Briggs of the *Mary Celeste* dismisses it as "ungodly superstition" in "The Chase." However, they're soon attacked by a Dalek.
- Novels, comics, and audio adventures have featured many dragons – often a subject for comedy. The Seventh Doctor mentions they exist in "Ghost Light." The dragon of Ace's first episode, "Dragonfire," is a biomechanoid assigned to keep the dragon fire away. The dragon of Ace's first episode, "Dragonfire," is a biomechanoid assigned to keep the dragon fire away. The Eighth Doctor rides one in *The Shadows of Avalon* to force a ceasefire between UNIT and the Fair Folk. The First Doctor drives a dragon off with a fire extinguisher in a comic about the Pied Piper. A dragon is the guardian of the Vault of Plenty on Gemino, and asks riddles for passage. In another short story, the Doctor beats a dragon in a cooking contest in "Doctor Who: Destination Prague" *(Doctor Who Short Trips)*.
- "The Doctor, the Widow and the Wardrobe" and "A Christmas Carol" both feature the Doctor having Christmas adventures with young children to bring them hope and happiness. Matt Smith describes "The Snowmen" noting "it does the sort of wonderful Doctor Who-ey Christmas things, you know, snow, aliens, good will, good cheer, someone trying to take

155

over the world. Hopefully it makes for good Christmas day telly" (Weintraub).

▶◀ The *2007 Annual* offers the Tenth Doctor story "Through the Rabbit Hole," in which Rose and the Doctor find themselves lost in a fairytale theme park gone wrong. After sorting everything out, the Doctor tells Rose that he can't make up stories; that's something he leaves to humans.

Music

▶◀ Introducing the "Doctor Who Proms," Davies notes that "music can go anywhere, reach anyone, and make better people of us all. Just like the Doctor." In writing the episode, Davies expressed hope that "this mini-adventure [would show] that music can take any shape or form, whether it's singing, or playing the recorder, or even the spoons." In his own introduction, the Tenth Doctor writes "Ode to the Universe" based on the music of the spheres.

▶◀ Each Doctor has had a tie to the world of music: the First Doctor disguises himself as a lyre player in "The Romans." The Second Doctor plays the recorder, the Fifth Doctor the harp, and the Seventh the spoons. The Sixth Doctor sings opera and the Third sings a lullaby on at least one occasion. The Fourth Doctor sings sharply enough to shatter glass in "The Power of Kroll." The Tenth Doctor admires the Beatles, and the Eighth, Puccini, while the Eleventh hires Stevie Wonder to sing for River and takes her to the "singing towers." Several Doctors go dancing with their companions.

▶◀ Fans adored the Tenth Doctor's Cast and Crew parting music video for "I'm Gonna Be (500 Miles)" and David Tennant, John Barrowman, and Catherine Tate's "The Ballad of Russell and Julie" with delightful rewritten lyrics concerning the show's reboot. Both are available on YouTube.

- Davies used the Rogue Traders song "Voodoo Child" to inspire his reborn Master. The lyric, "Here it comes, the sound of drums," provides the title and the song features in the episode.
- "Daleks in Manhattan" features Gershwin's "Rhapsody in Blue" and Irving Berlin's "Puttin' on the Ritz."
- In "Evolution of the Daleks," "Happy Days Are Here Again" by Milton Ager and Jack Yellen is heard on the radio.
- The Cyberconversion process going on to "The Lion Sleeps Tonight" on Pete's World adds an even more disturbing twist to the horrific scene.
- Rose refers to Cassandra as "Michael Jackson" in both of her appearances.
- In "The Girl in the Fireplace," the Tenth Doctor swings in, singing "I Could Have Danced All Night."
- "The Doctor Dances" sets the mood with Glenn Miller songs "In the Mood" and "Moonlight Serenade."
- "Closing Time" is likely named for the Semisonic song. ,In "The Age of Steel," the marching horde of mind-controlled people, called "sheep" by the Doctor reflects Pink Floyd song "Sheep" where the sheep are slaughtered in the "valley of steel." Both story and the song's album, *Animals* feature Battersea Park with a floating pig in one and floating airship in the other. Pink Floyd in turn incorporates *Doctor Who* theme music into its song "One of These Days."
- The "iPod" (actually a jukebox) that Cassandra unveils in "The End of the World" plays the "classical music" "Tainted Love" by Soft Cell and later "Toxic" by Britney Spears. This is appropriate as she is a tainted, toxic individual.
- "Father's Day" plays hits from 1987: "Never Gonna Give You Up" performed by Rick Astley and "Never Can Say Goodbye" performed by The Communards. Both have ties to Rose and Pete's relationship.

- In "42," Martha must answer a security question on who sold more records – Elvis Presley or The Beatles.
- The mysterious cubes Amy and Rory study can stop people's hearts, shoot lasers, and play the Chicken Dance.
- In "Hide," The Doctor quotes "Birds do it, bees do it, even educated fleas do it" from "Let's Do It, Let's Fall in Love" by Cole Porter.
- In "Asylum of the Daleks," the opera *Carmen* floods over the speakers, to everyone's surprise.

> DALEK SUPREME: What is the noise? Explain! Explain!
> DOCTOR: It's me.
> RORY: I'm sorry, what?
> DOCTOR: It's me, playing the triangle. Okay, I got buried in the mix. Carmen, lovely show. ("Asylum of the Daleks")

Carmen is actually a tragic tale in which the heroine dies at the end. Also, in the Habanera aria playing, Carmen describes herself as like smoke, untouchable and unattainable. Just like Oswin, who's playing it.

- The first human base on Mars is called Bowie Base One, a shout out to David Bowie's "Life on Mars."
- Trock Rock, short for "Time Lord Rock" is spreading through fandom. Like Harry Potter's "Wizard Rock," it's a kind of filk – fan-written songs about their favorite *Doctor Who* characters, often compared to modern folksinging. Wizard Rocker Amber Opsincs explains the workings of these independent bands, noting: "I play in libraries and book shops and even clubs. Most of my most recent shows have been at Harry Potter conventions. Anyone can come see a show of mine, I'm very family-friendly" (qtd. in Frankel 157). Alex Day (nicknamed Nerimon) was inspired to start Trock Rock based on the wizard rock phenomenon, along with his friends Charlie McDonnell, Liam Dryden, and "Ginger

Chris" Beattie. They began the indie rock band Chameleon Circuit in 2008, and now there are many more, available on the web for the most part. As with Wizard Rock, the band names are delightfully fannish:

- A Little More Sonic
- Absorb The Vortex
- Bad Wolf Bay
- Big Blue Box TV House Band
- Binary Nine
- Biological Meta-Crisis
- Blast!
- Blue Box Boys
- Children Of Time
- Companion
- Doctor Dolls
- Doctor Noise
- Exterminate!
- Friends Of The Ood
- Gallifrey and the Time Lords
- Gallifrey Girls
- Harmonies In Whoville
- Harriet Jones and the Former Prime Ministers
- Heart of the TARDIS
- It's A Sonic Screwdriver
- JellieBaby
- K-9's Frisbee
- Lonely Assassins
- Milkman Invasion of Earth
- Mr Saxon
- One Man, Two Hearts
- PARADOX
- Polyphase Avitron
- Project Indigo (YouTube)

- Psychic Paper
- Quantum Locked
- ReTARDIS
- RWR!
- Shadow Proclamation
- Slytheen Sisters
- Sol III
- Spatio Temporal Hyperlink
- TARDIR
- The Bad Wolves
- The Cult of Skaro
- The Doctor's Daughter
- The Forgotten Companion
- The Girls In The Fireplace
- The Lone Traveler
- The Lonely Traveler
- The Medusa Cascade
- The Noble Sisters
- The Odd Ood
- The Silent Philosopher
- The Skasas Paradigm
- The Timey-Wimey Device
- Time Vortexology
- Timey Wimey Malfunction
- Timey Wimey Stuff
- Tin Dog
- Tom Milsom
- Torchwood Institute
- Turn Left
- Unearthly Child
- Void Stuff
- Vortex
- Weevil Rock You

Games

► The Doctor visits the real-life London 2012 Olympic Games, when he saves the torch in the Eleventh Doctor minisode "Good as Gold" and lights the Olympic flame in the Tenth Doctor episode "Fear Her."

► "The Unicorn and the Wasp" is clearly based partially on the board game Clue ("Cluedo" in the UK), as in the library Professor Peach demands, "What are your doing with that lead piping?" The chief suspects correspond to the boardgame characters – Colonel Mustard (Colonel Curbishley), Professor Plum (Professor Peach), Reverend Green (Reverend Golightly), Miss Scarlett (Miss Redmond), Mrs. Peacock (Lady Eddison), and Mrs. White (Miss Chandrakala) . Many of the game's weapons and locations are also represented.

► Mickey reveals that he learned to fly a zeppelin on playstation ("Flesh and Steel")

► The Third Doctor makes the Master wait while he finishes a game of checkers, and notes, "The trouble with this game is that it's too simple. In any case, I'm more used to playing three-dimensional chess" ("The Mind of Evil").

► In "The Power of Three," the Doctor falls in love with the Wii.

► Clyde is skilled at video games, which he apparently can use to save the world in one of his final adventures:

> CLYDE: What's all this about? It looks like a big arcade game.
> RANI: This is what controls the nuclear fuel rods.
> CLYDE: It's just like a James Bond movie. Pull out the rods, close down the reactor, save the world.
> RANI: Only it's more like James Bond meets Mario.
> CLYDE: Which is ace, because I'm brilliant at Mario.
> RANI: If we don't do this right, Clyde, we don't just go back to the last level.
> (They use the joysticks to target the rods on the screen.) (SJA: "Sky" part two)

161

Other Series that Reference the Doctor

Doctor Who is referenced on *The Simpsons*, *The Big Bang Theory*, *Futurama*, *Buffy the Vampire Slayer*, *Criminal Minds*, *Green Courage*, *Better off Ted*, *Extras*, *The Venture Brothers*, *Sirens*, *Robot Chicken*, *Young Justice*, *Chelmsford 123*, *The Middleman*, *The Rugrats*, *Coupling*, *The Muppet Show*, *Beavis and Butthead*, *G.B.H.*, *CSI: New York*, *Dead Ringers*, *South Park*, *Mr. Bean*, *NCIS*, *The iCarly*, *Q*, *Phineas and Ferb*, *CSI: New York*, *The Vicar of Dibley*, *Emu's Broadcasting Company*, *The Two Ronnies*, *End of Part One*, *The Krankies*, *Eureka*, *The Suite Life of Zack and Cody*, *Spaced*, *Boy Meets World*, *Grey's Anatomy*, *Free Agents*, *Criminal Minds*, *Red Dwarf*, *Family Guy*, and *The Office*. Perhaps the TARDIS flies by or someone makes a police box quip. Someone dresses as the Fourth Doctor with his iconic scarf, or mentions the sort of geeks who watch *Doctor Who*.

- *My Little Pony: Friendship is Magic* famously has the recurring pony Dr. Hooves who suggests the Tenth Doctor. He's marked with an hourglass, and on one of the comic book covers, he's wearing the Fourth Doctor's scarf, holding the fob watch, and standing in front of a Weeping Angel statue. Fans have created ponies of all the other Doctors as well.
- In *Star Trek: The Next Generation*'s "The Neutral Zone," those who look at Claire Raymond's family tree very carefully will see a list of *Doctor Who* actors.
- In Davies' *Queer as Folk*, Vince makes *Doctor Who* references often, and finally receives a K-9 replica for his birthday.
- The *Supernatural* episode "The Girl Next Door" famously has a Kitsune named Amy Pond.
- On "Merry Christmas, Mr. Bean," a Dalek zaps a lamb in the Christmas pageant and saves the baby Jesus from a Tyrannosaurus.

- Daleks mingle with a crowd of other robots in *Looney Toons: Back in Action.*
- In a glance to the future, Cartman's buddy is the robot dog K10.
- Bill and Ted have their excellent adventures in a phone box.
- In the Cartoon Network show *Codename: Kids Next Door,* the nerdy children enjoy the show "Doctor Time Space and the Continuum."
- The web series *Epic Rap Battles of History* pitted the Doctor against *Back to the Future* icon Doc in 2012.
- *Leverage's* "Mile-High Job," features the two lead characters (played by Timothy Hutton and Gina Bellman) catching a plane. Timothy Hutton reads off the list of aliases: "Peter Davison, Sylvester McCoy and Tom Baker." Also, Gina Bellman's character has a Sarah Jane Baker ID.
- On 21 September 2010, Stephan Colbert put up an image of the Beast to represent Satan.
- In one episode of *The Sarah Silverman Program,* the character Brian buys a DVD boxset of "Dr. Lazer Rage." Dr. Rage is actually played by Christopher Eccleston, who shows up, coming to life on the cover of the box. There's also a blue telephone box, which is used to make a call.
- Darth Vader was pitted against a Dalek, a Cyberman and Colin Baker as the Sixth Doctor in a *Top Gear* sketch to see who was the fastest "Master of the Universe." Vader helped the Cyberman put its helmet on, but was exterminated by the Dalek (who was angry that it couldn't fit in the car). David Tennant was a guest later on.
- The TARDIS and Fourth Doctor have breezed by on *Futurama.* Also, the *Futurama* comic #32 is a direct *Doctor Who spoof,* with an alien Doctor (Zoidberg) and Deacons who shout "Excommunicate! Excommunicate!"

163

- *DangerMouse*, a British cartoon, has the heroes time travel through "a time-traveler's potting shed" and in other episodes they play with the words "Doctor Who?" suggesting they can't remember the answer.
- In the *American Dad!* episode "Escape from Pearl Bailey," the goth Debbie runs for Student Council President and must win over the *Doctor Who* club, all in a variety of iconic costumes.
- *Pinky and Perky*'s "Doctor Roo" features the Tenth Doctor as a kangaroo battling the Robo-Sheep.

- The British comedy series *The Goodies* suggested using the TARDIS as an actual telephone box to "phone home."
- In the Christmas Special finale of *Extras*, Darren Lamb tells his friend Andy that he's been offered a part in "the BBC's jewel in the crown, *Doctor Who*," but Andy dismisses the show as "camp, frothy nonsense." After five months out of work, Andy succumbs and plays a slug-like alien opposite David Tennant.
- *The Invisible Man* (2000) has several in the first episode: The main character is introduced to Doctors "Baker, McGann, Hartnell, and Troughton." Then he uses a torn calling card inscribed "I.M. Forman," the owner of the junkyard where the Doctor lives in "An Unearthly Child." There's also a magazine lying around with articles titled "Time and Relative Dimensions in Space" and "Winning the Game of Rassilon."
- On *Community*, Abed Nadir, who has Asperger's syndrome and dreams of making documentaries, loves playing "Inspector Spacetime," as he pretends to be an "infinity knight" in a bowler hat.

The series is also referenced in children's novels, including Christopher Paolini's novel, *Brisingr*, *High Wizardry* by Diane Duane and Rick Riordan's *The Serpent's Shadow*. And for the more scholarly fans, TARDIS and Dalek are in the *Oxford*

English Dictionary.

Computer games are packed with subtle references. *Fallout: New Vegas* has an add-on (Old World Blues) with a skeleton in a space helmet crying "Hey! Who turned out the lights?" *RuneScape* features NPC's Amelia and Rory, who prefer their hero in a bow tie, while "The Professor," an NPC in *Wizard 101,* offers around jelly babies and has a red telegraph box labeled "Warning: Smaller on the inside than the outside" and a Cosmic Calliper, rather than a screwdriver. *World of Warcraft* features a quest item called the "Ultrasonic Screwdriver." Daleks cameo in computer games from the 80s to present, including *Robot Odyssey, Roland in Time, Paradroid, Space Quest I* (the remake), *Beneath a Steel Sky, Boppin', Adventure Quest. Borderlands 2, Fallout, Lemmings 2: The Tribes, Team Fortress 2,* and *Apollo Justice: Ace Attorney.*

Comic book cameos include *The League of Extraordinary Gentlemen, Fantastic Four, Century: 1969, Century: 2009, Alf, Buffy the Vampire Slayer,* and *Speciale Martin Mystère.* British comic *Poot!* features Desmond Hoo, who *believes* he's the Doctor. A Dalek cameoes in the *Star Wars* comic strip, *Fett Club.* In the fan-produced *Star Wars* reference guide *Book of Imperial Shuttle Plans: Cygnus Spaceworks,* Skaro, Delta Magna and Cygnus appear. The Doctor has also appeared in several prose novels based in the Marvel Universe and several crossover characters have entered his universe and theirs. For instance, in an issue of *The Spectacular Spider-Man* utilizing alternate realities and time travel, the words "BAD WOLF" can be seen on an alley wall.

Steven Moffat's Comic Relief show, *Doctor Who and the Curse of Fatal Death,* may be the most famous parody. The frequently-killed Doctor is played by Rowan Atkinson, Joanna Lumley, Hugh Grant, Richard E. Grant and Jim Broadbent, with Jonathan Pryce as the Master. On November 13, 1999, BBC Two did an entire "Doctor Who Night" with sketches by Mark Gatiss (these are included as extras in the DVD box set *Doctor Who: The Beginning*). On *Dead Ringers,* comedian Jon Culshaw often impersonated the Fourth Doctor and made unscripted calls as him, even calling four of the original actors. When it became a television show, Culshaw continued to play the Fourth Doctor, then in 2005 added spoofs of the new show to his repertoire.

In books, *Doctor Whom: E.T. Shoots and Leaves* by A. R. R. R. Roberts, author of *The Soddit*, is a parody crossover of *Doctor Who* with the grammar guide *Eats, Shoots & Leaves* by Lynne Truss. *Barry Trotter and the Unnecessary Sequel* (2003) features Doctor Loo, a time traveling wizard with his device the POTTY. The *Dalek Survival Guide* parodies *The Worst-Case Scenario Survival Handbooks,* while *Return of the Bunny Suicides* and *Dawn of the Bunny Suicides* see the rabbits using the TARDIS to aid their quest. There are many YouTube parodies and mash-ups as well. Unfortunate references to Doctor Poo and the Turdis across television and other media sink the references to a more juvenile level...or occasionally a far more adult one.

Additional parodies have appeared on the Michael Bentine sketch show *It's a Square World* (beginning in December 1963), followed by *Late Night with Conan O'Brien, Dave Allen at large, Crackerjack, The Lenny Henry Show French & Saunders Victoria Wood As Seen On TV, The Real McCoy, Fast Forward, Saturday Night Live, Shooting Stars, The Charlotte Church Show, The Harry hill Show, Chewin' the Fat,* and *The Friday Night Project* (several of these sketches were released as extras on *Doctor Who and the Curse of Fatal Death*). In addition, stars like David Tennant and Catherine Tate have occasionally guested on the shows, bringing extra laughs to all (David Tennant also visited *The Catherine Tate Show* itself). *The Late Late Show with Craig Ferguson* has featured Matt Smith, Alex Kingston and Karen Gillan.

Finally, a *Doctor Who* appearance at the 2012 Olympics was trimmed to a brief TARDIS sound, based on time constraints. But he was there, at least in spirit.

Where to Take Your Who Tour

Many fans don't just write about their love for *Who* – They journey to Britain! With tours in London and Wales, fans can stroll where Rose buys her chips, or visit the last police box. Iconic locations feature in much of the series, as Big Ben is demolished by aliens and Buckingham Palace nearly follows suit. Most of the shooting takes place in South Wales, where fans can find even more locations, from the bar of Rory's stag night to 13 Bannerman Road and the actual Bad Wolf Bay. Moviemaps.org and Doctorwholocations.net have even more locations than the ones below. And don't forget Stonehenge, site of the Pandorica.

London

- Big Ben – apparently it's been repaired after all the invasions
- Buckingham Palace – ditto
- The London Eye, home of the Nestene Consciousness on their first adventure
- The Doctor Who Shop and Museum in east London
- Forbidden Planet London Megastore (for *Doctor Who* Products)
- The famous Earls Court police box
- The 7th floor Sky Bar at The Grange St Paul's Hotel where the Doctor and Clara have drinks in "The Bells of Saint John." It has views of St Paul's Cathedral and The Shard.
- Trafalgar Square, where Rose and Mickey have lunch by a fountain in "Rose"

- The Brandon Estate, in Kennington and the Wallis House in Brentford, posing as the Powell Estate, served as the location of the Tylers' flat.
- Wharton Street & St. Mary Street features a chariot driver in "The Wedding of River Song." Rose can be seen there in her season one arrival and season two exit, and this is the corner where Donna Noble tries to hail a cab in her wedding gown.
- Rose and the Doctor run across the Westminster Bridge to the London Eye in "Rose." In "Aliens of London," the alien spacecraft lands in the Thames right by the bridge. Clara and the Doctor ride across here in "The Bells of Saint John."
- The new Shakespeare's Globe Theatre, opened in 1997 as a reconstruction of the original, which was destroyed by fire in 1613, rebuilt, and torn down in 1644. *Doctor Who* became the first television drama to film there.
- *Doctor Who* also became the first television drama to film atop the Tower of London.

Wales
- Work on "Rose" began on July 20th 2004 at Howell's department store, posing as Henrik's. This location was used repeatedly for Henrick's and other department stores.
- Rose's father dies outside St Paul's Church in Grangetown, Cardiff, which serves as St Christopher's.
- Cardiff Royal Infirmary – Albion Hospital in "Aliens of London," the WWII hospital of "The Doctor Dances." Also used in TW: "Fragments" and "Turn Left."
- The Temple of Peace in Cathays Park provided the majority of the sequences aboard Platform One in "The End of the World" and scenes in the Sibylline temple of Pompeii. Scenes from SJA: "Mona Lisa's Revenge" also took place there. It hosted the German restaurant River Song crashes in "Let's Kill Hitler" the Silurian senate

chamber of "Cold Blood," and the chamber filled with dead senators in "Gridlock."

- An unused area of the National Museum of Wales in Cardiff became van Statten's exhibit room. This is the show's go-to museum, also seen in "The Lazarus Experiment," "Planet of the Dead," SJA: "Mona Lisa's Revenge," "Vincent and the Doctor," and "The Big Bang."
- The interiors for Van Stattan's and the British government's compound in "The Christmas Invasion" were filmed in Cardiff's Millennium Stadium, as were interior scenes for "The Pandorica Opens," "The Impossible Astronaut"/"Day of the Moon," and "A Good Man Goes to War."
- Southerndown Beach, in Ogmore Vale near Bridgend, is the alien planet seen in the opening of "Army of Ghosts" and also functions as Darlig Ulv Stranden: Bad Wolf Bay.
- The Former Ely Paper Mill is the Nestene Base in "Rose," hospital in "New Earth," Cyber factory in "The Age of Steel," and expressway entrance in "Gridlock."
- Mir Steel is used for the chess game of "The Wedding of River Song," the mining operation of "The Hungry Earth" and "Cold Blood," the town in "A Christmas Carol," the execution site on the Crucible in "Journey's End," the ship in "Planet of the Dead," and the food truck location in "The End of Time."
- The principal stand-in for Royal Hope Hospital of "Smith and Jones" was the School of Sciences at the University of Glamorgan in Pontypridd.
- Amy & Rory's house is at 6 Bute Esplanade.
- The Ninth Doctor and Rose have chips on Queen Street and watch Dickens at the New Theatre.
- Cardiff High School and houses on Clinton Road do most scenes for *The Sarah Jane Adventures*.
- At St. Gwynno's Church, Amy and Rory see their older selves ("Cold Blood"/"The Hungry Earth")

- Pirate scenes for "The Curse of the Black Spot" took place on the actual ship the Phoenix.
- Llandaff Cathedral provided the war memorial, as well as the setting for John Smith and Joan Redfern's imaginary wedding.
- The major location for "School Reunion" was Duffryn High School in Newport.
- St Fagans National History Museum ("Human Nature," "The Family of Blood")
- The Craig Y Nos Castle, featured in "Tooth and Claw" as Torchwood House
- Barry Island Heritage Railway ("The Empty Child"/"The Doctor Dances")
- National Botanic Garden of Wales ("The Waters of Mars")
- Plantasia Botanic Gardens ("Cold Blood")
- Llandaff Cathedral (Vincent and the Doctor)
- Cyfarthfa Castle ("Let's Kill Hitler")
- Brangwyn Hall ("Let's Kill Hitler," "The Big Bang)
- Castell Coch ("The Vampires of Venice")
- Skenfrith Castle ("Amy's Choice")
- St. Mary's Church (SJA: "Lost In Time")
- Llancaiach Fawr Manor ("The Vampires of Venice")
- Cardiff Castle is the Monastery of "The Rebel Flesh" and "The Almost People," the crypt of "The Name of the Doctor" and the prison Vastra visits in "The Name of the Doctor."
- Cardiff's Glamorgan House posed as the Town Hall in "Boom Town," while Mermaid Quay offered scenes in the square.
- For "Silence in the Library"/"Forest of the Dead," Hensol Castle, at Hensol in the Vale of Glamorgan, posed as the CAL hospital. Donna plays with her fictional children in Victoria Park. Donna and Lee's wedding photo is taken at St Mary's of Angels. Brangwyn Hall in Swansea provided the Library's main

entrance, while Swansea Library itself was the main location.

- Captain Jack's frantic dash to the TARDIS in "Utopia" takes place at Millennium Square in Cardiff Bay.
- The Vicarage provides the exterior of Amy's house, where little Amelia waits all night.
- The Doctor returns Sarah Jane, Mickey, Jack and Martha to Earth on their final joint adventure at Morgan Jones Park in Caerphilly
- Broadfell Prison was actually Caerphilly Castle. The same location was used for "The Rebel Flesh"/"The Almost People" "The Vampires of Venice," Henry VIII's Bedroom, the UNIT Lab exterior, Cumbria Monastery in "The Bells of Saint John," and the site of the Doctor's chess game in "Nightmare in Silver."
- The Doctor pursues the Master on the Cardiff Docks.
- Much of "The Doctor, the Widow and the Wardrobe" was at Stradey Castle.
- In St. Augustine's Church, Wilf sees the TARDIS in the stained glass window in "The End of Time."
- Hensol Castle hosted scenes for "Closing Time" and "The Wedding of River Song"
- Howell's/House of Fraser are the stores of "Closing Time."
- Neath Abbey is the doppelgänger chamber in "The Rebel Flesh" and "The Almost People." It's the control room of "The Beast Below" and the church crypt of "Vincent and the Doctor." It's also the UNIT lab in "The Power of Three."
- Cefn Llwyd is the lake of "The Unicorn and the Wasp."
- Donna's wedding reception scenes of "The Runaway Bride" were filmed at the Baverstock Hotel in Merthyr Tydfil. The wedding took place at St John the Baptist Church in Cardiff on the 14th. The TARDIS/car chase sequence took place on Ely Link Road in Cardiff. Donna's wedding two years later was filmed at St Mary's Church in Marshfield.

171

Wales: Dining and Lodging

- La Fosse restaurant stood in for Tizzano's Pizza Restaurant in "Rose."
- Doctor and Blon's dinner was taped in and around Bistro 10 on Mermaid Quay in Cardiff Bay.
- Cassandra's party was actually held at the Bar Orient restaurant on Cardiff Bay.
- The Doctor and Wilf's café in "The End of Time" is actually the Kardomah Cafe in Swansea
- The alien bar scene where the Doctor bids farewell to Captain Jack and Alonso Frame before dying takes place at Tiger Tiger in Cardiff. This bar is used for many bar scenes, including those in TW: "Kiss Kiss Bang Bang" and "Partners in Crime."
- Eddie's Diner is the café of "The Impossible Astronaut," also used in series seven.
- Canton Delaware is picked up by government agents at Le Monde in "The Impossible Astronaut."
- Bowls Inn is the site of Rory's stag party.
- Manor Parc Hotel and Seabank Hotel were used for "The God Complex."
- The Plan Cafe and Penarth Kebab and Pizza also appear in Series Seven.

VALERIE ESTELLE FRANKEL

What Remains to be Said?

Moffat shows often have particular tropes mixed with the terror. Most of his episodes are psychological horror, evoking fear through creepy images rather than violence or death. His monsters involve masks (Clockwork Men, Empty Child) and statues/mannequins (Weeping Angels, Smilers). His aliens, from those in spacesuits to the Silence with no mouths and the body-swapping Great Intelligence, are faceless drones of a sort. He also has a tendency to make the most innocuous things absolutely terrifying, like the voice of a child asking for his mother, clock ticks, statues, shadows, birdsong, mirrors, a crack in the wall... and now, after making almost everything else scary, the silence itself terrifying. He wants to leave his audience with no place to hide.

Davies was less known for horror. He calls the climax of "The Stolen Earth," at which a Dalek ray shoots the Doctor, who begins to regenerate, a satire of romance fiction and joked that seminal films such as *Gone with the Wind* should have ended with a Dalek shooting the male lead ("Friends and Foe"). He calls the reunion between Rose and the Doctor to "The biggest romance [the viewer] has ever seen," though it lasts only seconds. Tennant described the Doctor's wounding as a "moment of high emotion" and lamented that "[the Doctor] can't have a happy moment, especially with a cliffhanger needing to be written" ("Friends and Foe"). Of course, Rose and Ten's romance ends with her receiving a replacement Doctor – the tragic parting of Series Two has been rewritten with an implausible, slapped-on, too-perfect ending.

These two writers, blending their different styles, have created a fandom of TARDIS-sized proportions, creating a

173

mixture of dark fairytales and bright science fiction, blending terrors of the television with an adoration of books and reading. The fandom has exploded as a result, crafting a world of fanfiction, art, and culture, much like *New Who's* creators. Here's to another fifty years!

List of Doctors and Companions

The Doctor (s):

1. William Hartnell 1963 - 1966
2. Patrick Troughton 1966 - 1969
3. Jon Pertwee 1970 - 1974
4. Tom Baker 1974 - 1981
5. Peter Davison 1981 - 1984
6. Colin Baker 1984 - 1986
7. Sylvester McCoy 1987 - 1989
8. Paul McGann (1996 movie + audio productions)
9. Christopher Eccleston 2005
10. David Tennant 2005 - 2009
11. Matt Smith 2010 - 2013
?. John Hurt 2013
12. Peter Capaldi 2014

Principal Companions:

Carole Ann Ford as Susan Foreman 1963 - 1964
Jacqueline Hill as Barbara Wright 1963 - 1965
William Russell as Ian Chesterton 1963 - 1965
Maureen O'Brien as Vicki 1965
Adrienne Hill as Katarina 1965
Jean Marsh as Sara Kingdom 1965
Peter Purves as Steven Taylor 1965 - 1966
Jackie Lane as Dodo (Dorothea) Chaplet 1966
Anneka Wills as Polly 1966 - 1967
Michael Craze as Ben Jackson 1966 - 1967
Fraser Hines as Jamie McCrimmon 1966 - 1969

Deborah Watling as Victoria Waterfield 1967 - 1968
Wendy Padbury as Zoe Heriot 1968 - 1969
Caroline John as Liz Shaw 1970
Katy Manning as Jo Grant 1971 - 1973
Elisabeth Sladen as Sarah Jane Smith 1973 - 1976
Ian Marter as Surgeon Lt Harry Sullivan, RN 1974 - 1975
Louise Jameson as Leela 1977 - 1978
Mary Tamm as Romana 1978
Lalla Ward as Romana 1979 - 1981
Matthew Waterhouse as Adric 1980 - 1982
Sarah Sutton as Nyssa 1981 - 1983
Janet Fielding as Tegan Jovanka 1981 - 1984
Mark Strickson as Turlough 1983 - 1984
Nicola Bryant as Peri Brown 1984 - 1986
Bonnie Langford as Melanie Bush 1986 - 1987
Sophie Aldred as Ace 1987 - 1989
Daphne Ashbrook as Doctor Grace Holloway 1996
Billie Piper as Rose Tyler 2005 - 2006
Bruno Langley as Adam Mitchell 2005
John Barrowman as Jack Harkness 2005
Noel Clarke as Mickey Smith 2006
Freema Ageyman as Martha Jones 2007
Catherine Tate as Donna Noble 2008
Karen Gillan as Amy Pond 2010 - 2012
Arthur Darvill as Rory Williams 2010 - 2012
Alex Kingston as River Song 2010 -2013
Jenna-Louise Coleman as Clara Oswin Oswald 2012 –

Whoniverse Episode Guide

First Doctor (William Hartnell) Seasons 1-3 1963-1965

001. An Unearthly Child
002. The Daleks
003. The Edge of Destruction
004. Marco Polo
005. The Keys of Marinus
006. The Aztecs
007. The Sensorites
008. The Reign of Terror
009. Planet of Giants
010. The Dalek Invasion of Earth
011. The Rescue
012. The Romans
013. The Web Planet
014. The Crusade
015. The Space Museum
016. The Chase
017. The Time Meddler
018. Galaxy 4
019. Mission to the Unknown
020. The Myth Makers
021. The Daleks' Master Plan
022. The Massacre of St Bartholomew's Eve
023. The Ark
024. The Celestial Toymaker
025. The Gunfighters
026. The Savages
027. The War Machines

028. The Smugglers
029. The Tenth Planet

Second Doctor (Patrick Troughton) Seasons 4-6 1966-1968
030. The Power of the Daleks
031. The Highlanders
032. The Underwater Menace
033. The Moonbase
034. The Macra Terror
035. The Faceless Ones
036. The Evil of the Daleks
037. The Tomb of the Cybermen
038. The Abominable Snowmen
039. The Ice Warriors
040. The Enemy of the World
041. The Web of Fear
042. Fury from the Deep
043. The Wheel in Space
044. The Dominators
045. The Mind Robber
046. The Invasion
047. The Krotons
048. The Seeds of Death
049. The Space Pirates
050. The War Games
051. Spearhead from Space
052. Doctor Who and the Silurians
053. The Ambassadors of Death
054. Inferno

Third Doctor (Jon Pertwee) Seasons 7-11 1970-1973
055. Terror of the Autons
056. The Mind of Evil
057. The Claws of Axos
058. Colony in Space
059. The Dæmons
060. Day of the Daleks

061. The Curse of Peladon
062. The Sea Devils
063. The Mutants
064. The Time Monster
065. The Three Doctors
066. Carnival of Monsters
067. Frontier in Space
068. Planet of the Daleks
069. The Green Death

Fourth Doctor (Tom Baker) Seasons 12-18 1974-1980
070. The Time Warrior
071. Invasion of the Dinosaurs
072. Death to the Daleks
073. The Monster of Peladon
074. Planet of the Spiders
075. Robot
076. The Ark in Space
077. The Sontaran Experiment
078. Genesis of the Daleks
079. Revenge of the Cybermen
080. Terror of the Zygons
081. Planet of Evil
082. Pyramids of Mars
083. The Android Invasion
084. The Brain of Morbius
085. The Seeds of Doom
086. The Masque of Mandragora
087. The Hand of Fear
088. The Deadly Assassin
089. The Face of Evil
090. The Robots of Death
091. The Talons of Weng-Chiang
092. Horror of Fang Rock
093. The Invisible Enemy
094. Image of the Fendahl
095. The Sun Makers

096. Underworld
097. The Invasion of Time
098. The Ribos Operation
099. The Pirate Planet
100. The Stones of Blood
101. The Androids of Tara
102. The Power of Kroll
103. The Armageddon Factor
104. Destiny of the Daleks
105. City of Death
106. The Creature from the Pit
107. Nightmare of Eden
108. The Horns of Nimon
109. The Leisure Hive
110. Meglos
111. Full Circle
112. State of Decay
113. Warriors' Gate
114. The Keeper Of Traken
115. Logopolis

Fifth Doctor (Peter Davison) Seasons 19-21 1982-1984
116. Castrovalva
117. Four To Doomsday
118. Kinda
119. The Visitation
120. Black Orchid
121. Earthshock
122. Time-Flight
123. Arc of Infinity
124. Snakedance
125. Mawdryn Undead
126. Terminus
127. Enlightenment
128. The King's Demons
129. The Five Doctors
130. Warriors Of The Deep

131. The Awakening
132. Frontios
133. Resurrection of the Daleks
134. Planet of Fire
135. The Caves of Androzani

Sixth Doctor (Colin Baker) Seasons 22-23 1985-1986
136. The Twin Dilemma
137. Attack of the Cybermen
138. Vengeance On Varos
139. The Mark of The Rani
140. The Two Doctors
141. Timelash
142. Revelation of the Daleks
143. The Trial of a Time Lord
        The Trial of a Time Lord: The Mysterious Planet
        The Trial of a Time Lord: Mindwarp
        The Trial of a Time Lord: Terror of the Vervoids
        The Trial of a Time Lord: The Ultimate Foe

Seventh Doctor (Sylvester McCoy) Seasons 24-26 1987-1989
144. Time and the Rani
145. Paradise Towers
146. Delta and the Bannermen
147. Dragonfire
148. Remembrance of the Daleks
149. The Happiness Patrol
150. Silver Nemesis
151. The Greatest Show in the Galaxy
152. Battlefield
153. Ghost Light
154. The Curse of Fenric
155. Survival

Eighth Doctor (Paul McGann) 1996
156 Doctor Who Television Movie (The Enemy Within)

Old Series Numbering	New Who	Modern Numbering
Series 1 2005	**Ninth Doctor and Rose Tyler**	
157	Rose	1.1
158	The End of the World	1.2
159	The Unquiet Dead	1.3
160	Aliens of London	1.4
	World War Three	1.5
161	Dalek	1.6
162	The Long Game	1.7
163	Father's Day	1.8
164	The Empty Child	1.9
	The Doctor Dances	1.10
165	Boom Town	1.11
166	Bad Wolf	1.12
	The Parting of the Ways	1.13
	Children in Need	Short
Series 2 2006	**Tenth Doctor and Rose Tyler**	
167	The Christmas Invasion	Christmas Special
168	New Earth	2.1
169	Tooth and Claw	2.2
170	School Reunion	2.3
171	The Girl in the Fireplace	2.4
172	Rise of the Cybermen	2.5
	The Age of Steel	2.6
173	The Idiot's Lantern	2.7
174	The Impossible Planet	2.8
	The Satan Pit	2.9
175	Love & Monsters	2.1
176	Fear Her	2.11
177	Army of Ghosts	2.12
	Doomsday	2.13

Series 3 2007	Tenth Doctor and Martha Jones	
178	The Runaway Bride	Christmas Special
179	Smith and Jones	3.1
180	The Shakespeare Code	3.2
181	Gridlock	3.3
182	Daleks in Manhattan	3.4
	Evolution of the Daleks	3.5
183	The Lazarus Experiment	3.6
184	42	3.7
185	Human Nature	3.8
	The Family of Blood	3.9
186	Blink	3.1
187	Utopia	3.11
	The Sound of Drums	3.12
	Last of the Time Lords	3.13
	Time Crash	Short
	Voyage of the Damned	Christmas Special
Series 4 2008	Tenth Doctor and Donna Noble	
189	Partners in Crime	4.1
190	The Fires of Pompeii	4.3
191	Planet of the Ood	4.2
192	The Sontaran Stratagem	4.4
	The Poison Sky	4.5
193	The Doctor's Daughter	4.6
194	The Unicorn and the Wasp	4.7
195	Silence in the Library	4.9
	Forest of the Dead	4.1
196	Midnight	4.8
197	Turn Left	4.11
198	The Stolen Earth	4.12

199	Journey's End	4.13
200	The Next Doctor	Christmas Special
201	The Planet of the Dead	Easter Special
202	The Waters of Mars	Fall Special
203	The End of Time	Christmas and New Year Specials
Series 5 2010	**Eleventh Doctor and Amy Pond**	
203	The Eleventh Hour	5.1
	Meanwhile in the TARDIS	Short
204	The Beast Below	5.2
205	Victory of the Daleks	5.3
206	The Time of Angels	5.4
	Flesh and Stone	5.5
	Meanwhile in the TARDIS 2	Short
207	The Vampires of Venice	5.6
208	Amy's Choice	5.7
209	The Hungry Earth	5.8
	Cold Blood	5.9
210	Vincent and the Doctor	5.10
211	The Lodger	5.11
212	The Pandorica Opens	5.12
	The Big Bang	5.13
213	A Christmas Carol	Christmas Special
	Space/Time	Short
Series 6 2011	**Eleventh Doctor, Amy Pond, Rory Williams**	
214	The Impossible Astronaut	6.1
	Day of the Moon	6.2
215	The Curse of the Black	6.3

	Spot	
216	The Doctor's Wife	6.4
217	The Rebel Flesh	6.5
	The Almost People	6.6
218	A Good Man Goes to War	6.7
219	Let's Kill Hitler	6.8
	Night and the Doctor	5 Shorts
220	Night Terrors	6.9
221	The Girl Who Waited	6.10
222	The God Complex	6.11
223	Closing Time	6.12
224	The Wedding of River Song	6.13
225	The Doctor, the Widow and the Wardrobe	Christmas Special
	Pond Life	5 Shorts

Series 7 2012-2013	**Eleventh Doctor, Amy Pond, Rory Williams, Clara Oswald**	
226	Asylum of the Daleks	7.1
227	Dinosaurs on a Spaceship	7.2
228	A Town Called Mercy	7.3
229	The Power of Three	7.4
230	The Angels Take Manhattan	7.5
231	The Snowmen	Christmas Special
232	The Bells of Saint John	7.6
233	The Rings of Akhaten	7.7
234	Cold War	7.8
235	Hide	7.9
236	Journey to the Centre of the Tardis	7.10
237	The Crimson Horror	7.11

238	Nightmare in Silver	7.12
239	The Name of the Doctor	7.13
240	The Day of the Doctor	50th Anniversary

Torchwood
Series 1 2006

Everything Changes	1.1
Day One	1.2
Ghost Machine	1.3
Cyberwoman	1.4
Small Worlds	1.5
Countrycide	1.6
Greeks Bearing Gifts	1.7
They Keep Killing Suzie	1.8
Random Shoes	1.9
Out of Time	1.10
Combat	1.11
Captain Jack Harkness	1.12
End of Days	1.13

Series 2 2008

Kiss Kiss, Bang Bang	2.1
Sleeper	2.2
To the Last Man	2.3
Meat	2.4
Adam	2.5
Reset	2.6
Dead Man Walking	2.7
A Day in the Death	2.8
Something Borrowed	2.9
From Out of the Rain	2.10
Adrift	2.11
Fragments	2.12
Exit Wounds	2.13

2009 Miniseries
Children of Earth

5 parts

2011 Miniseries
Miracle Day

10 parts

The Sarah Jane Adventures
Series 1 2007

Invasion of the Bane	New Year's Special
Revenge of the Slitheen	1.1-1.2
Eye of the Gorgon	1.3-1.4
Warriors of Kudlak	1.5-1.6
Whatever Happened to Sarah Jane?	1.7-1.8
The Lost Boy	1.9-1.10

Series 2 2008

The Last Sontaran	2.1-2.2
The Day of the Clown	2.3-2.4
Secrets of the Stars	2.5-2.6
The Mark of the Berserker	2.7-2.8
The Temptation of Sarah Jane Smith	2.9-2.10
Enemy of the Bane	2.11-2.12

Series 3 2009

From Raxacoricofallapatorius with Love	Short
Prisoner of the Judoon	3.1-3.2
The Mad Woman in the Attic	3.3-3.4
The Wedding of Sarah Jane Smith	3.5-3.6
The Eternity Trap	3.7-3.8
Mona Lisa's Revenge	3.9-3.10
The Gift	3.11-3.12

Series 4 2010

The Nightmare Man	4.1-4.2
The Vault of Secrets	4.3-4.4
Death of the Doctor	4.5-4.6
The Empty Planet	4.7-4.8
Lost in Time	4.9-4.10
Goodbye, Sarah Jane Smith	4.11-4.12

Series 5 2011

Sky	5.1-5.2
The Curse of Clyde Langer	5.3-5.4
The Man Who Never Was	5.5-5.6

Additional Specials

Dr. Who and the Daleks (Peter Cushing as the Doctor) 1965

Daleks' Invasion of Earth 2150 A.D (Peter Cushing as the Doctor) 1966

Shada, Unfinished episode released later on DVD (Fourth Doctor and Romana) 1979

K-9 and Company: A Girl's Best Friend (Sarah Jane Smith) 1981

Dimensions in Time, Crossover with EastEnders (Jon Pertwee, Tom Baker, Peter Davison, Colin Baker and Sylvester McCoy as the Doctor plus many of the companions) 1993

Doctor Who and the Curse of Fatal Death (Rowan Atkinson, Joanna Lumley, Hugh Grant, Richard E. Grant and Jim Broadbent as the Doctor) 1999

Death Comes to Time, webcast (Seventh Doctor and Ace) 2001

Real Time, webcast (Sixth Doctor) 2002

Scream of the Shalka (Richard Grant as the Doctor) 2003

Attack of the Graske (Tenth Doctor and Rose short) 2005

Tardisodes, one minute introductions to each Series Two episode (Tenth Doctor and Rose), 2006

The Infinite Quest (Tenth Doctor and Martha) 2007

Music of the Spheres (Tenth Doctor short) 2008

Dreamland (Tenth Doctor) 2009

K-9, animated show (John Leeson as K-9) 2009-2010.

"500 miles" and "The Ballad of Russell and Julie," music videos (Tenth Doctor and cast and crew) 2010

Death is the Only Answer (Eleventh Doctor short) 2011

The Doctor's Clothes (Eleventh Doctor short) 2011

Good as Gold (Eleventh Doctor short) 2012

The Night of the Doctor (Eighth Doctor short) 2013

Bibliography

Primary Sources
BBC Press Release "Michelle Ryan and Lee Evans to Star in
First Doctor Who Special of 2009" *BBC* 23 Jan 2009.
http://www.bbc.co.uk/pressoffice/pressreleases/stories/20
09/01_january/23/doctor.shtml.

Colville, Robert. "Russell T Davies Doctor Who interview: full
transcript." *The Daily Telegraph* 11 April 2009.
http://blogs.telegraph.co.uk/news/robertcolvile/9445447/
Russell_T_Davies_Doctor_Who_interview_full_transcript.

Cook, Benjamin. "Matt Smith is the Eleventh Doctor." *Doctor
Who Magazine* February 2009. http://whoismattsmith.com.

Davies, Russell T. "Alien Resurrection." *The Guardian* 13 June
2005. Belam.

--. *Damaged Goods*. UK: London Bridge, 1996.

--. Interview: Writer Russell T Davies (Century Falls) *Cult TV*
2005.
http://www.bbc.co.uk/cult/classic/centuryfalls/interview.s
html.

--. "Interview - Writer Russell T Davies" (Dark Season) *Cult*.
2005.
http://www.bbc.co.uk/cult/classic/darkseason/interview.s
html.

--. "Transmission Was Madness. Honestly." *The Guardian* 15
Sept 2003.
http://www.theguardian.com/media/2003/sep/15/channel
4.gayrights.

Davies, Russell T. and Benjamin Cook. *Doctor Who: The Writer's
Tale: The Untold Story of the BBC Series*. UK: Random House,
2008.

Doctor Who: The Complete Fifth Series (2010; BBC Home Entertainment, 2010), DVD.

Doctor Who: The Complete First Series (2005; BBC Home Entertainment, 2005), DVD.

Doctor Who: The Complete Fourth Series (2008; BBC Home Entertainment, 2008), DVD.

Doctor Who: The Complete Second Series (2006; BBC Home Entertainment, 2006), DVD.

Doctor Who: The Complete Seventh Series (2013; BBC Home Entertainment, 2012), DVD.

Doctor Who: The Complete Sixth Series (2011; BBC Home Entertainment, 2011), DVD.

Doctor Who: The Complete Third Series (2007; BBC Home Entertainment, 2007), DVD.

"Fool if You Think It's Over," Featurette, *Joking Apart*, Series 1. DVD.

"Friends and Foe". *Doctor Who Confidential.* Series 4. Episode 12. 28 June 2008. BBC.

Gaiman, Neil. "Q & A: Neil Gaiman" *The Guardian* 16 May 2011. Belam.

Gatiss, Mark "Doctor Who's Mark Gatiss: Why I wanted to bring back the Ice Warriors." *Radio Times* 13 April 2013. http://www.radiotimes.com/news/2013-04-13/doctor-whos-mark-gatiss-why-i-wanted-to-bring-back-the-ice-warriors.

"An Interview with Gareth Roberts." *BBC* 17 September 2011. http://www.bbc.co.uk/mobile/tv/doctorwho/news/news_17092011/index.shtml.

Lane, Andy. *All-Consuming Fire.* UK: London Bridge, 1994.

Masters, Tim. "Meet the 11th Doctor: Matt Smith" *BBC News* 2 April 2010. http://news.bbc.co.uk/2/hi/entertainment/8580985.stm.

Moffat, Steven, *Doctor Who Magazine* (Royal Tunbridge Wells, Kent: Panini Comics) 7 March 2013.

"Open All Hours." *Doctor Who Confidential. Doctor Who: The Complete Sixth Series.*

Parkin, Lance. *The Gallifrey Chronicles.* UK: Random House, 2005.

Pryor, Cathy. "Russell T Davies: One of Britain's Foremost Television Writers." *The Independent* 22 Oct 2006.

Radish, Christina. "Steven Moffat Talks *Doctor Who*, His Favorite Upcoming Episodes, Writing the Doctor and Sherlock Holmes, the 50th Anniversary, and More." *Collider* 2013. http://collider.com/steven-moffat-doctor-who-season-7-interview/

--. "Matt Smith, Jenna Coleman and Steven Moffat Talk *Doctor Who*, Smith Leaving the Show, and Preparing for a New Doctor." *Collider* 2013 http://collider.com/doctor-who-matt-smith-jenna-coleman-interview.

The Sarah Jane Adventures: The Complete Fifth Season (BBC Home Entertainment, 2012), DVD.

The Sarah Jane Adventures: The Complete First Season (2008; BBC Home Entertainment, 2008), DVD.

The Sarah Jane Adventures: The Complete Fourth Season (2011; BBC Home Entertainment, 2011), DVD.

The Sarah Jane Adventures: The Complete Second Season (2009; BBC Home Entertainment, 2009), DVD.

The Sarah Jane Adventures: The Complete Third Season (2010; BBC Home Entertainment, 2010), DVD.

Torchwood: The Complete First Season (2008; BBC Home Entertainment, 2007), DVD.

Torchwood: The Complete Second Season (2008; BBC Home Entertainment, 2008), DVD.

Soghomonian, Talia. "*Doctor Who* Producer Piers Wenger Exclusive Interview; Talks About the Fifth Series, the New Doc and Filming in America." *Collider* 2009. http://collider.com/piers-wenger-interview-doctor-who.

Weintraub, Steve. "Matt Smith Talks *Doctor Who* Series 7 Part Two, the Show's 50th Anniversary, the Return of Neil Gaiman, and More." *Collider* 2012. http://collider.com/matt-smith-doctor-who-season-7-interview.

"The World of Who." *Doctor Who Confidential. Doctor Who: The Complete First Series.*

Secondary Sources

Akers, Laura Geuy. "Empathy, Ethics, and Wonder." Lewis, Courtland and Smithka 145-156.

The Beginner's Guide to Doctor Who. BBC. http://www.bbc.co.uk/doctorwho/classic/guide.shtml.

Belam, Martin, Ed. *Who's Who? The Resurrection of the Doctor (Guardian Shorts).* UK: Guardian Books, 2011. Kindle Edition.

Berger, Richard. "Screwing Aliens and Screwing with Aliens: Torchwood Slashes the Doctor." *Illuminating Torchwood: Essays on Narrative, Character and Sexuality in the BBC Series,* ed. Andrew Ireland. Jefferson, NC: McFarland, 2010. 66-78.

Britton, Piers D. *TARDISbound.* New York: IB Tauris, 2011.

Burdge, Anthony. *The Mythological Dimensions of Doctor Who.* 2nd ed. MythInk Books. Kindle Edition. 2013.

Burke, Jessica. "Doctor Who and the Valkyrie Tradition, Part 2: Goddesses, Battle-demons, Witches, & Wives." Burdge 140-182.

Cawley Christian. "Alwyn Turner on Terry Nation." *Kastrerborous* 27 Dec 2011. http://www.kasterborous.com/2011/12/alwyn-turner-on-terry-nation.

--. "Neil Gaiman Writes Nothing O'Clock for 50th Anniversary eBook Range." *Kastrerborous* 5 Nov 2013. http://www.kasterborous.com/2013/11/neil-gaiman-writes-nothing-oclock-50th-anniversary-ebook-range.

Chapman, James. *Inside the Tardis: The Worlds of Doctor Who.* USA: I.B. Tauris, 2006.

Charles, Alec. "War without End?: Utopia, the Family, and the Post-9/11 World in Russell T. Davies's 'Doctor Who.'" *Science Fiction Studies* 35, no. 3 (November 2008): 450-465. Academic Search Complete.

Child, Ben. "Doctor Who's Matt Smith Materialises at Comic-Con." *The Guardian* 25 July 2011. Belam.

Collis, Clark. "The Doctor is In." *Entertainment Weekly* no. 1218 (August 3, 2012): 28-35. Academic Search Complete.

--. "Doctor Who?" *Entertainment Weekly* 1272/1273 (2013): 16. Academic Search Complete.

Cooper, Steven and Kevin Mahoney. *Steven Moffat's Doctor Who 2010: The Critical Fan's Guide to Matt Smith's First Series (Unauthorized)* London: Punked Books, 2011.

--. *Steven Moffat's Doctor Who 2011: The Critical Fan's Guide to Matt Smith's Second Series (Unauthorized)* London: Punked Books, 2012.

Cornell, Paul, Keith Topping, and Martin Day. *The Discontinuity Guide: The Definitive Guide to the Worlds and Times of Doctor Who.* Texas: MonkeyBrain Books, 2004.

Deller, Ruth. "What the World Needs Is…a Doctor." Lewis, Courtland and Smithka 239-247.

Dipaolo, Marc Edward. "Political Satire and British-American Relations in Five Decades of Doctor Who." *Journal of Popular Culture* 43, no. 5 (October 2010): 964-987. *Academic Search Complete.*

Dixit, Priya. "Relating To Difference: Aliens and Alienness in Doctor Who and International Relations." *International Studies Perspectives* 13.3 (2012): 289-306. Academic Search Complete.

Flickett, Travis. "IGN: The Stolen Earth Review." *IGN TV.* 1 Aug 2008. http://www.ign.com/articles/2008/08/01/doctor-who-the-stolen-earth-review.

Frankel, Valerie Estelle. *Harry Potter, Still Recruiting: An Inner Look at Harry Potter Fandom.* USA: Zossima Press, 2012.

Geraghty, Lincoln. "From Balaclavas To Jumpsuits: The Multiple Histories And Identities Of Doctor Who's Cybermen." *Atlantis* 30.1 (2008): 85-100. Academic Search Complete.

Graham, Elaine L. *Representations of the Post/Human: Monsters, Aliens and Others in Popular Culture.* New Brunswick: Rutgers University Press, 2002.

Hale, Kelly. "Timing Malfunction: Television Movie + the BBC Eighth Doctor Novels = a Respectable Series." Stanish and Myles.

Harvey, C. B. "Canon, Myth, and Memory in Doctor Who."
Burdge 22-35.

Hickman, Clayton, ed. *The Brilliant Book of Doctor Who 2012*.
London: BBC Books, 2011.

Hoskin, Dave. "The New Man: The Regeneration Of Doctor
Who." Metro 169 (2011): 130. MasterFILE Complete.

Jenkins, Henry. *Textual Poachers*. New York: Routledge, 1992.

Kenney, Doug. "Spoilers." *National Lampoon* 1, no. 13 (April
1971).

Layton, David. "Closed Circuits And Monitored Lives:
Television as Power in *Doctor Who*." *Extrapolation* (Kent
State University Press) 35.3 (1994): 240-251. Academic
Search Complete.

--. *The Humanism of Doctor Who*. Jefferson, NC: McFarland, 2012.

Lewis, Courtland and Smithka. *Doctor Who and Philosophy: Bigger
on the Inside*. USA: Open Court, 2010.

Martin, Dan. "The Mind Robber: Doctor Who Classic Episode
#4" *The Best Doctor Who Episodes of All Time*. *The Guardian*
March 28, 2013. http://www.guardian.co.uk/tv-and-
radio/tvandradioblog/2013/mar/28/the-mind-robber-
doctor-who.

McFarland, Melanie. "On TV: BBC America's Hot 'Torchwood'
is a Cool Place to be Saturday Nights." *Seattle Post-Intelligencer*
12 September 2007.
http://seattlepi.nwsource.com/tv/330634_tv07.html.

McLean, Gareth. "Steven Moffat: The Man with a Monster of a
Job: Steven Moffat on the Challenges of Running *Doctor
Who*." *The Guardian* 22 Mar 2010. Belam.

Mead, Laura. "David Tennant's Bum." Stanish and Myles.

Merritt, Stephanie. "Tennant's Extra." *The Observer* 11 Dec.
2005. Belam.

Miles, Tat, and Lawrence Wood, *About Time, The Unauthorized
Guide to Doctor Who, Volume 1*. USA: Mad Norwegian Press,
2006.

Mulkern, Patrick. "Doctor Who Premiere – New Title
Sequences, Matt Smith on Twitter and a Big Surprise." *Radio
Times* 15 Aug 2012.

http://www.radiotimes.com/blog/2012-08-15/doctor-who-premiere---new-title-sequences-matt-smith-on-twitter-and-a-big-surprise.

Newman, Kim. *Doctor Who*. UK: British Film Institute, 2005.

Nussbaum, Emily. "Fantastic Voyage." *New Yorker* 88.16 (2012): 126-127. Academic Search Complete.

Ruediger, Ross. "*Doctor Who*: Why Peter Capaldi Is the Ideal 12th Doctor" *Vulture* 5 Aug 2013. http://www.vulture.com/2013/08/doctor-who-why-capaldi-is-the-ideal-12th-doctor.html.

Schuster, Marc and Tom Powers. *The Greatest Show in the Galaxy: The Discerning Fan's Guide to Doctor Who*. Jefferson, NC: McFarland, 2007.

Sharma, Iona. "All the Way Out to the Stars." Stanish and Myles.

Short, Sue. "Doctor Who and Star Trek: Twenty-First Century Reboots." *Cult Telefantasy Series*. Jefferson, NC: McFarland and Co., 2011. 166-194.

Sleight, Graham. *The Doctor's Monsters: Meanings of the Monstrous in Doctor Who*. USA: I.B. Tauris, 2012.

Stanish, Deborah and L.M. Myles. Eds. *Chicks Unravel Time: Women Journey Through Every Season of Doctor Who*. Mad Norwegian Press. Kindle Edition.

Tulloch, John and Manuel Alvarado. *Doctor Who: The Unfolding Text*. London: Macmillan, 1983.

Wilkins, Alasdair. "The Bells of Saint John." *AV Club* 30 Mar 2013. http://www.avclub.com/articles/the-bells-of-saint-john,95443.

Glossary of Terms and Abbreviations

Arc, arc stories: A storyline that lasts through multiple episodes, like River and the Doctor's backwards romance or the crack in Amy's wall, shown in each episode of Series Five.

BBC: Station that distributes *Doctor Who,* classic and modern. BBC publishing also produces much supplementary nonfiction and published the Eighth Doctor Adventures and Past Doctor Adventures.

Big Finish Productions: Publisher of audio adventures starring many of the original *Who* actors from 1999 onwards.

Blog: Short for "Weblog," an online journal that may discuss pop culture.

Canon: This term refers to material designated "official" or "sanctioned by the author or producer" contrasted with other authors' contributions to a franchise (The *Star Wars* movies, for instance, are considered canon; the novels and comics are not).

Classic *Doctor Who* (*Old Who*): The show lasted from 1963 to 1989, with a television movie in 1996. It included the first eight Doctors, the TARDIS, and short multi-part adventures. The first two Doctors' eras were filmed in black and white, and a number of these episodes are missing.

Companions: *New Who* Companions of the Ninth and Tenth Doctor include Rose Tyler, Jack Harkness, Mickey Smith, Martha Jones, and Donna Noble. Companions of the Eleventh include Amy Pond, Rory Williams, River Song, and Clara Oswald.

Conventions: Fannish gatherings. Comic-Con in San Diego is the largest and most famous, while there are Comic-Con branches appearing in many other locations. Gallifrey One and Chicago TARDIS are top *Who* conventions.

Cosplay: Short for "costume play." Wearing costumes and occasionally acting them out.

Crossover fiction: Fan fiction, fan art, etc. that combines more than one series, such as *Doctor Who* and *Star Trek*.

Davies: Russell T Davies was responsible for reviving the show and remained in charge from 2005-2009 during the Tenth and Eleventh Doctors' eras, series 1-4.

Doctor Who Magazine: The most well-known fan production, running from 1979 through now.

Doctor: Considered the same character, though played by different actors, with different personalities. His name is unknown.

DVDs: Most *Doctor Who* episodes have been released this way, including *New Who, Old Who* individual episodes, and sometimes the only remaining fragments of missing episodes as part of a larger themed collection. Cartoon episodes and parodies are also available on DVD.

Expanded Universe: Refers to the novels, comics, audio adventures, games, parodies, and other "semicanon" or "noncanon" material, in contrast with the television show.

Fan art: Noncommercial art based on the series and frequently posted on the web to share with other fans.

Fan communities: These could refer to fan groups that meet in person or on the web.

Fan fiction: Also called "fanfic." Noncommercial fiction based on the series and generally posted on the web.

Fan groups: Social groups (usually organized by region and meeting in person) devoted to activities and discussion of the series.

Fan service: Scenes intended to please longtime fans rather than tell a strong story.

Fan sites: Websites devoted to the show often containing news, encyclopedias, discussion boards, or fan art and fan fiction. The TARDIS Data Core is the largest repository of information, while *Doctor Who Online, Doctor Who.com, WhovianNet,* many forums and Facebook pages fill the web.

IDW Comics: American producer of *Doctor Who* comic books and graphic novels

K-9: Beloved robot dog of the Fourth Doctor era, also seen in "School Reunion" and some of *The Sarah Jane Adventures*. The attempted spinoff *K-9 and Company* only had a pilot, and the Australian show *K9* lasted two years.

Minisode: Episode continuations (usually only five minutes) that were filmed for Children in Need or various promotional specials and are generally included on the DVDs. These were particularly made in the Tenth and Eleventh Doctor eras to take advantage of new media. Most are available on YouTube.

Missing Episodes: Many episodes from the black and white era were discarded. Only in 1978 was an effort made to collect them by the BBC Film and Videotape Library. In 1983, a total of 134 episodes (sections of original 4-parters or other multipart serials) were missing, believed lost, and by the 50th anniversary in 2013, 97 episodes were still undiscovered. A few have been recreated using audio recordings, original promotional stills, and cartoons.

MMO: A Massively Multiplayer Online game, which can also function as a fannish community

Moffat: Steven Moffat wrote some episodes during Davies' reign, and then took over the show with the Eleventh Doctor.

New Doctor Who (*New Who*): The 2005 show is in a modern one-hour format, with Christmas specials, minisodes, and other experimental forms as well. It has heavy story arcs through each year.

New Series Adventures: *New Who* books aimed at kids

Novelizations: Generally an adaptation of the same story in a novel medium – the novelization of the popular episode "Genesis of the Daleks" contains extra material, but is basically the same adventure.

NPC: A Non Player Character in a computer game – someone written in who functions as part of the story.

Podcasts: A form of internet radio, with many Who fansites.

Puffin: For the Fiftieth Anniversary, Puffin ebooks is releasing eleven authors' short stories, one for each Doctor.

Retcon: Retroactive Continuity Change, contradicting a fact that was previously established. *Torchwood* humorously invents the drug "retcon" to aid them in this practice.

RPG: Role Playing Game such as *Dungeons and Dragons*. There are *Doctor Who* versions.

The Sarah Jane Adventures (SJA): A 2007 spin-off based off the *Doctor Who* episode "School Reunion," in which beloved companion Sarah Jane Smith (Elisabeth Sladen) from original *Who* returns but prefers to adventure on earth. It's a children's show as she outwits aliens with the help of her adopted teen children and their neighborhood friends. The show was unfortunately canceled with the actress's death in 2011.

Season: In the US this refers to a year of a show. In the UK, this term used to be used (and thus, is used to refer to, say, season 19 of the old show) but no longer is.

Series: The current name for a year of a show in the UK. Thus, *New Who* is divided into series 1 through 7. The show went from Season 26 to a television movie to Series 1, technically speaking.

Shipping: Writing, creating art, etc. devoted to a particular relationship between characters.

Ships: Short for relationships; a popular term used in fan fiction.

Slash: Refers to romantic homosexual relationships not evident in the series (such as Harry Potter and Draco Malfoy, or the Doctor and the Master). This is a popular genre of fanfiction.

Speculative Fiction: An all-encompassing name for science fiction and fantasy.

Target: Publishers of the original novelizations and *The Companions of Doctor Who.*

Torchwood (TW): A 2006 spin-off from *Doctor Who,* managed by Davies. It follows the adventures of the Torchwood 3 team in Cardiff as they hunt aliens. It had two years, then the five-part miniseries *Torchwood: Children of Earth,* then a year on

Starz as *Torchwood: Miracle Day* in 2011. All four series starred John Barrowman as Captain Jack Harkness and Eve Myles as Gwen Cooper.

Transcripts: Written form of the audio/visual recordings. A full fan-created set of all fifty years of episodes is available at *Chrissie's Transcripts Site* at Chakoteya.net.

Trock Rock: Short for Time Lord Rock. Independent bands write songs about *Doctor Who* and its characters.

Virgin New Adventures: Continuing novels of the Seventh and Eighth Doctors published after the series ended in 1989.

Whoniverse: Fannish name for the fictional universe containing old and new *Doctor Who, Sarah Jane Adventures, Torchwood,* and often the Expanded Universe stories and fanfiction.

Youtube: www.YouTube.com. Most of the minisodes, and some cast and crew interviews are available free on Youtube, along with the David Tennant music videos.

Index

1963, 10, 24, 26, 117, 125, 127, 143, 166, 175

1984, 122

2000 AD, 149

28 Days Later, 145

50th anniversary, 30, 54, 127

666, 151

Ace, 52, 53, 72, 102, 109, 114, 130, 155, 165, 176

adipose, 49

Agatha Christie, 85, 128, 133

"Age of Steel," 41, 75, 103, 141, 144, 157, 169

Aldous Huxley, 125

Alex Kingston, 11, 27, 166, 176

Alice in Wonderland, 133

Alien, 91, 123

Alien Bodies, 111

"Aliens of London," 15, 106, 168

All-Consuming Fire, 126, 130

"The Almost People," 50, 102, 170, 171

Amy Pond, 10, 15, 20, 30, 31, 33, 38, 50, 54, 56, 60, 61, 69, 70-72, 82, 89, 92, 96, 98, 102, 103, 106-110, 119, 120, 121, 124-126, 135, 149, 158, 162, 169, 171, 176, 199

"Amy's Choice," 170

anagram, 34, 91, 103, 112

"The Angels Take Manhattan," 37, 38, 69, 124

"The Arc of Infinity," 50, 100

"Army of Ghosts," 85, 89, 101, 112, 138, 148, 169

Astrid Peth, 48, 91, 149

"Asylum of the Daleks," 18, 21, 158

Atlantis, 20, 37, 152, 153

ATMOS, 42, 113

Atraxi, 49, 106

Autons, 25, 39, 65, 95, 97

Avatar, 148

Avengers, 67

Back to the Future, 117, 145, 147, 163

"Bad Wolf," 39, 40, 44, 47, 85, 104, 110, 114, 141, 144, 167, 169

banana, 111, 147

Bannerman Road, 10, 113, 167

Barbara Wright, 85, 114, 139, 175

"Battlefield," 102

Battlestar Galactica, 121, 122

BBC, 10, 16, 18, 32, 37, 38, 52-56, 78, 88, 94, 110,

127, 139, 142, 150, 164, 165

"The Beast Below," 13, 15, 25, 101, 106, 120, 122, 135, 139, 171

The Beatles, 107, 156, 158

"The Bells of Saint John," 37, 44, 45, 69, 167, 168, 171

Bernice Summerfield, 32, 54, 112

"The Big Bang," 31, 100, 101, 119, 140, 149, 162, 169, 170

Big Ben, 48, 167

Big Brother, 40, 85, 122, 141

Big Finish Audio Productions, 24, 54, 55, 81, 84, 86, 90, 110, 111, 112, 133, 150

Billie Piper, 39, 53, 88, 176

Blade Runner, 122, 148

Blake's 7, 117, 143

"Blink," 63, 64, 81, 84, 102, 115

Blon, 49, 172

Blowfish, 106

Blue Peter, 99

"Boom Town," 14, 77, 104, 136, 170

bowtie, 67, 69

"The Brain of Morbius," 22, 128, 129

Brigadier Lethbridge-Stewart, 17, 47, 85, 93, 111, 113-114

The Brilliant Book 2012, 15, 28, 52, 71, 124, 153

Buck Rogers in the 25th Century, 145

Buffy the Vampire Slayer, 93, 140, 162, 165

Bunny Suicides, 166

Byzantium, 29, 138

C.S. Lewis, 33, 125, 126

camera, 46, 50, 87

Cardiff, 14, 18, 77, 80, 93, 168-172

Carmen, 158

Casablanca, 144

Casanova, 76, 80, 86-87, 90

Cassandra, 157, 172

Castrovalva, 91, 99

Catherine Tate, 132, 156, 166, 176

celery, 67, 97, 100

cellphones, 39, 41, 46, 55

Century Falls, 77, 79

Chalk, 81

"The Chase," 131, 155

chess, 161, 169, 171

Chicago TARDIS, 11, 200

Chicken Dance, 158

Children in Need, 69

Children of Earth, 88

Children's Ward, 80, 92

"A Christmas Carol," 32, 61, 62, 68, 83, 115, 123, 134, 137, 139, 148, 155, 169

"The Christmas Invasion," 25, 87, 103, 104, 106, 121, 147, 151, 169

Christopher and His Kind, 88

Christopher Eccleston, 14, 30, 39, 53, 67, 76, 80, 86, 103, 128, 163, 175

Clara Oswald, 16, 22, 25, 26, 28, 36, 37, 44, 50, 51, 71, 82, 91, 93, 98, 103, 108,

120, 124, 136, 147, 148, 167, 168, 176

Cloister Library, 19, 109

Clone Wars, 121

"Closing Time," 107, 125, 157, 171

Clyde, 22, 77, 115, 119, 121, 134, 148, 149, 161

"Cold Blood," 71, 97, 106, 107, 169, 170

"Cold War," 97

Cole Porter, 158

Colin Baker, 14, 43, 55, 127, 163, 175

Comic-Con, 10, 11, 30, 70

comics, 24, 27, 54, 109, 115, 116, 120, 129, 137, 153, 155

Community, 164

"Continuity Errors," 32, 83

Coronation Street, 142

costumes, 67-69, 79, 119, 130, 149

Coupling, 81-84, 162

cricket outfit, 67, 70, 100

"The Crimson Horror," 42, 91, 98

crossover, 54, 57, 117, 119, 139, 165, 166

Cthulhu, 126

The Curse of Fatal Death, 83, 94, 165, 166

"The Curse of Fenric," 91, 151

"The Curse of Peladon," 90, 97

"The Curse of the Black Spot," 51, 69, 84, 135, 152, 170

Cushing films, 109, 110, 120

Cybermen, 19, 37, 41, 49, 50, 75, 95, 96, 100, 101, 106, 107, 112, 118, 119, 122, 178

The Da Vinci Code, 144

"The Dæmons," 138, 150, 152

"Dalek," 97, 99, 104, 110, 145

Daleks, 9-10, 18-19, 23, 47-50, 54, 95-96, 106, 107, 110, 117, 121, 135, 139, 157, 163, 165

"Daleks in Manhattan," 135, 139, 157

Damaged Goods, 56, 79, 80

Dark Season, 77, 78, 80

David Tennant, 10, 11, 21, 42, 51, 55-59, 62, 67, 70, 76, 85-94, 100, 121-124, 128, 131, 132, 156, 163-164, 166, 173, 175

Davros, 19, 42, 43, 47, 110

"Day of the Moon," 98, 99, 103, 111, 134, 144, 169

The Day the Earth Stood Still, 122

"Dead Man Walking," 154

Dead Ringers, 162, 165

"The Deadly Assassin," 21, 128

death, 28, 48, 87, 93, 102, 107, 118-120, 123, 134, 137, 146, 150, 154, 173

"Death Is the Only Answer," 87

"Destiny of the Daleks," 23, 121, 153

Dickens, 58, 71, 107, 131, 134, 169

"Dinosaurs on a Spaceship," 94, 123, 149

Discontinuity Guide, 19, 109

"The Doctor Dances," 57, 81, 83, 104, 111, 118, 120, 134, 137, 148, 157, 168, 170

Doctor Who Magazine, 44, 54, 56, 75, 108, 110

Doctor Who movie, 10, 17, 20, 22, 24, 101, 118, 145, 148

Doctor Who Proms, 51, 156

Doctor Who: A History of the Universe, 19, 109

Doctor Who: A New Dimension, 86

Doctor Whom: E.T. Shoots and Leaves, 166

"The Doctor, the Widow and the Wardrobe," 75 126, 155, 171

"The Doctor's Clothes," 69, 87

"The Doctor's Daughter," 84, 151, 160

"The Doctor's Wife," 21, 23, 99, 100, 111, 121, 125, 128

Donna Noble, 13, 15, 27, 28, 48, 62, 63, 72, 79, 83, 90, 98, 103-105, 114, 122, 143, 146, 168-171, 176

"Doomsday," 32, 54, 103, 110, 124, 151

Douglas Adams, 24, 121, 140, 141

Dracula, 66, 80, 134, 146, 150

"Dragonfire," 34, 50

Dreamland, 55, 103, 114, 121, 123, 144

E.T., 148-149

EastEnders, 85, 139

Easter, 63, 64, 117, 136, 139

Eighth Doctor, 15, 17-18, 20, 24, 37, 54, 60, 68, 85, 98, 110-112, 120, 127, 129, 133, 145, 150, 152, *see also Doctor Who* movie

Einstein, 87

Eleventh Doctor, 11, 24, 31, 50-51, 54, 56, 60, 69, 70, 82, 84, 87, 92, 108, 113, 119-120, 124, 128, 130, 135, 137, 138, 146, 148, 152, 161

"The Eleventh Hour," 17, 20, 21, 49, 83, 84, 106, 124

Elisabeth Sladen, 78, 85-87, 93, 176

"The Empty Child," 71, 80, 81, 104, 111, 118, 134, 149, 153, 170, 173

"End of Days," 151

"The End of the World," 78, 101, 138, 157, 168

"The End of Time," 14, 23, 63, 75, 80, 87, 105, 112, 125, 143, 169, 171, 172

"The Enemy of the World," 17

The Enemy Within see Doctor Who movie

e-space, 150

"The Eternity Trap," 148

"Evolution of the Daleks," 142, 157

"Eye of the Gorgon," 113, 119, 134, 151

Face of Boe, 48, 105

Facebook, 45, 55

"The Family of Blood," 99, 105, 170

fan groups, 65

fan service, 48

fanfiction, 11, 24, 55-57, 62, 87, 174

"Father's Day," 14, 104, 157

"Fear Her," 25, 104, 161

fez, 68, 69, 101

Fifth Doctor, 11, 59, 67, 70, 84, 94, 97, 98, 100, 102, 112, 127, 133, 150, 156

Fiftieth Anniversary, 16, 54

Firefly,, 121

First Doctor, 22, 50, 66, 98, 101, 127, 131, 152-156

"The Five Doctors," 50, 95, 133

"Flesh and Steel," 161

"Flesh and Stone," 61, 106, 120

"Forest of the Dead," 27- 29, 81, 83, 108, 124, 170

Fourth Doctor, 19, 27, 34, 50, 60, 67, 70, 72, 78, 91, 98, 113, 121, 127, 133, 138, 143, 152, 153, 156, 162-165

"Fragments," 168

Francine Jones, 90, 105

Frankenstein, 68, 122, 128, 129, 132, 135, 145

Freema Agyeman, 89, 142

"From Out of the Rain," 42, 154

Frostfire, 154

Futurama, 142, 162-163

Gallifrey Chronicles, 35

Gallifrey One, 11, 199

Game of Thrones, 142,

games, 9, 54, 115, 161, 165

Gandalf, 115, 120, 124

Gareth Roberts, 56, 75, 78, 107, 111

Gelth, 49, 134, 137, 153

"Ghost Light," 72, 130, 137, 155

Ghostbusters, 148

"The Girl in the Fireplace," 81, 111, 137, 146, 157

"The Girl Who Waited," 92, 103

"The God Complex," 99, 142, 153, 172

Gone with the Wind, 173

"Good as Gold," 161

"A Good Man Goes to War," 14, 84, 107, 138, 169

The Graduate, 147

The Great Intelligence, 28, 95, 96, 153, 173

"The Greatest Show in the Galaxy," 51, 150

"The Green Death," 57

"Gridlock,"" 111, 139, 149, 169

Gulliver's Travels, 32

Gwen Cooper, 21, 48, 79, 89, 93, 122

H.G. Wells, 66, 122, 133

Hamlet, 87, 131, 132

Harold Saxon, 85, 91, 105, 114, 159

Harriet Jones, 16, 47, 48, 79, 80, 159

Harry Potter, 55, 90, 91, 115, 123, 124, 128, 148, 158, 221

Harry Sullivan, 150, 176

Henry Jenkins, 55-58, 62, 65
"Hide," 103, 138, 148, 158
Hitchhiker's Guide, 24, 121, 135, 141
"The Horror of Fang Rock," 128
"Human Nature," 17, 60, 75, 105, 110, 170
Hunger Games, 44
"The Hungry Earth," 106, 130, 169
I, Claudius, 94
Ian Chesterton, 26, 47, 114, 175, 176
Ice Warriors, 21, 97
"The Idiot's Lantern," 39, 42, 104
"Image of the Fendahl," 97, 128
"The Impossible Astronaut," 13, 90, 102, 107, 108, 111, 138, 143, 147, 169, 172
"The Impossible Planet," 104, 139, 151
Indiana Jones, 143, 145
"Inferno," 85, 97, 99, 118, 133
The Infinite Quest, 55
Internet, 16, 40, 45
Invasion of the Body Snatchers, 148
"The Invasion of Time," 50
Iris Wildthyme, 54
Izzy Sinclair, 120
Jack Harkness, 21, 42, 48, 57, 59, 71, 79, 80, 92, 95, 97, 99, 103, 105, 107, 112-114, 118, 120, 122, 134, 146, 148, 154, 157, 171, 172, 176

James Bond, 146, 161
Jamie McCrimmon, 32, 86, 100, 120, 175
Jason and the Argonauts, 155
Jaws, 146
Jekyll, 81, 82, 128, 129
jelly babies, 50, 98, 165
Jenna Coleman, 44, 91
Jo Grant, 46, 50, 92, 113, 114, 176
John Hurt, 123, 175
Joking Apart, 81, 82, 83
Jon Pertwee, 46, 66, 68, 127, 175
journal, 28, 29, 31
"Journey to the Centre of the Tardis," 25, 26, 50, 122, 124
"Journey's End," 14, 23, 47, 48, 93, 103, 169
Jubilee Pizza, 110
Judge Dredd, 149
Judoon, 49, 106, 152
Jurassic Park, 149
K-9, 85, 93, 122, 150, 162
Karen Gillan, 89, 91, 93, 166, 176
Kate Stewart, 93, 111
"The Keeper of Traken," 90
"Kiss Kiss Bang Bang," 80, 93, 106, 119, 172
Krillitanes, 49
Kursaal, 150
Lake Silencio, 56, 107
Lance Parkin, 19, 35, 109
The Land of Fiction, 32, 97, 152, 153
"The Last of the Time Lords," 14, 124, 136

"The Lazarus Experiment,"
53, 105, 139, 146, 149, 169

Leela, 72, 78, 133, 176

"Let's Kill Hitler," 30, 71, 83,
88, 94, 107, 111, 138, 147,
168, 170

The Lion King, 24, 147

"The Lodger," 56, 60, 61, 88,
106, 119

"Logopolis," 99

London, 10, 14, 19, 48, 65,
69, 83, 96, 99, 104, 126,
145, 153, 161, 167, 168

"The Long Game," 40, 104

"Lost in Time," 114, 137, 170

Loups-Garoux, 150

love, 27, 30, 56, 61, 76, 80,
82, 95, 107, 117, 140, 144,
145, 161, 167

Love and Monsters, 39, 64,
104-106

Lovecraft, 126

"Mad Woman in the Attic,"
113

Madame Kovarian, 52

Maleficent, 89

Managra, 34, 132, 153

The Manchurian Candidate, 144

Mark Gatiss, 84, 87, 91, 130,
165

Martha Jones, 14, 15, 48, 50,
55, 72, 79, 85, 89, 90, 98,
102, 103, 110, 112, 116,
123, 131, 139, 141, 146,
147, 158, 171, 176

Marvel, 149, 165

Mary Poppins, 115, 147

The Master, 22, 23, 31- 33,
47, 48, 57, 90, 91, 94, 98,
100, 101, 103, 105, 111,
120, 123-125, 134, 137,
138, 145, 150, 157, 161,
165, 171

Matt Smith, 11, 24, 30, 68,
69, 70, 86-88, 92, 128,
146, 155, 166, 175, 192

"Meanwhile in the
TARDIS," 61

Men in Black, 142, 144

Merlin, 150

Mickey Smith, 15, 16, 103,
116, 122, 144, 161, 167,
171, 176

"Midnight," 14, 48, 90, 105,
132, 144, 151

"The Mind of Evil," 46, 47,
133, 161

"The Mind Robber," 25, 32,
37, 196

Mine All Mine, 76, 79

Minotaur, 152-153

Miracle Day, 137

Missing Adventures, 24, 53

missing episodes, 16-17

Momento, 144

"Mona Lisa's Revenge," 149,
168, 169

Monty Python, 27, 140

music, 156-157

myth, 150-155

"The Name of the Doctor,"
22, 28, 50, 108, 124, 131,
170

Narnia, 33, 125, 126

NASA, 114

Neil Gaiman, 23, 88, 99, 109,
110, 121, 125, 128

Nestene, 106, 167, 169

New Adventures, 24, 53, 56,
80, 110

New Series Adventures, 54

news, 39, 41, 105

"The Next Doctor," 17, 78, 95, 123, 140

Nicholas Briggs, 56

"The Night of the Doctor," 15, 112

"Night Terrors," 25, 32, 52, 107, 110, 139, 146

"Nightmare in Silver," 23, 128, 171

Ninth Doctor, 9-10, 18, 22, 39, 40, 53, 63, 75, 80, 93, 101, 111, 121, 128, 136, 137, 169

novelizations, 11, 17, 24, 33, 53, 57

Nyssa, 100, 112, 176

Olympics, 161, 166

Ood, 14, 49, 105, 142

Oxford English Dictionary, 165

Pandorica, 14, 15, 29, 31, 84, 92, 98, 102, 106, 107, 118, 124, 150, 167, 169

"The Pandorica Opens," 31, 84, 92, 102, 107, 118, 124, 169

parody, 57, 62, 83, 165, 166

"The Parting of the Ways," 100, 124

"Partners in Crime," 30, 172

Past Doctor Adventures, 54

Patrick Troughton, 66, 68, 90, 127, 164, 175

Paul Cornell, 14, 56, 84

Paul McGann, 18, 66, 85, 127, 140, 148, 164, 175

Peri Brown, 43, 133, 176

Pete's World, 41, 157

Peter Capaldi, 88, 89, 175

Peter Davison, 59, 66, 86, 100, 127, 163, 175

Peter Pan, 135

petrichor, 125

Phantom of the Opera, 128, 135

"Planet of the Dead," 46, 61, 86, 105, 136, 139, 143, 151, 169

"Planet of the Ood," 142

Pompeii, 72, 89, 135, 141, 146, 168

The Poseidon Adventure, 143

"The Power of Kroll," 156

"The Power of Three," 31, 45, 93, 111, 158, 161, 171

Press Gang, 81, 82, 84

Prime Minister, 48

"Prisoner of the Judoon," 149

Professor Yana, 90

Proms, *see Doctor Who* Proms

psychic, 61, 97

Puffin short stories, 54, 127

"Pyramids of Mars," 57, 72, 91, 101, 114, 128, 151

Queen Victoria, 61, 71, 104, 135

Queer as Folk, 76-80, 162

radio, 44, 129, 157

Rani Chandra, 73, 77, 93, 137, 148

Rassilon, 80, 164

reality TV, 9, 14, 15, 20, 31, 33, 34, 38, 40, 41, 116, 130, 133, 141, 142, 154

"The Rebel Flesh," 148, 170, 171

Red Dwarf, 142, 162

regeneration, 20, 21, 22, 23, 138, 173

religions, 136

"Remembrance of the Daleks," 52, 96

"Reset," 110

retcon, 18, 20, 21

"Revelation of the Daleks," 42

"Revenge of the Cybermen," 19

"The Rings of Akhaten," 25, 36, 37, 120

"Rise of the Cybermen," 41, 75, 91, 104, 116

River Song, 13, 22, 27- 31, 38, 48, 56, 60, 69, 71, 82, 83, 94, 97-100, 106-108, 119, 124, 138, 145, 146, 153, 156, 168-171, 176

"The Robots of Death," 76, 128, 143

Romans, 84, 98, 107

Romana, 23, 92, 152, 153, 176

Rory Williams, 20, 33, 38, 54, 69, 87, 92-95, 98, 102-103, 106-108, 119, 121, 123, 126, 143, 146, 158, 165, 167, 169, 172, 176

"Rose," 39, 53, 97, 106, 167, 168

Rose Tyler, 10, 15, 16, 20, 30, 39, 40, 48, 50, 53, 56-57, 63, 70-71, 76, 78-80, 91, 97, 100-105, 107, 110, 118, 124, 135, 137, 149, 153, 156-157, 167-169, 172, 173, 176

"The Runaway Bride," 25, 85, 105, 122, 171

Russell T Davies, 9, 10, 14, 30, 39, 46, 48, 56, 57, 67, 76-83, 86, 87, 91-94, 101, 103, 105, 111, 112, 117, 120, 121, 123, 133, 143, 144, 156, 157, 162, 173

Sam Jones, 110, 120

Santa, 9, 68, 137

Sarah Jane, 10-11, 35, 37, 72, 73, 77, 85, 92, 98, 105, 112-114, 119, 137, 153, 163, 171, 176, 193

The Sarah Jane Adventures, 10, 22, 73, 77, 78, 85, 106, 113, 115, 121, 144, 151, 169

The Sarah Silverman Program, 163

"The Satan Pit," 13, 91, 104, 136, 151

"School Reunion," 78, 85, 93, 104, 170

science fiction, 9, 14, 22, 27, 35, 37, 52, 53, 60, 68, 76, 79, 82, 88, 89, 108, 115-118, 122, 125, 128, 133, 140, 174

Scottish, 100, 135

Scream of the Shalka, 55, 86, 90, 93

Second Doctor, 11, 19, 23, 32, 66, 68, 90, 96- 98, 100, 102, 127, 152, 156

"The Seeds of Death," 178

"The Seeds of Doom," 73

Seven Keys to Doomsday, 90, 110

Seventh Doctor, 17, 27, 33-34, 51, 53, 60, 68, 80, 90,

110, 127, 130, 150, 151, 155

Shada, 33, 54, 121

Shadow Proclamation, 48, 160

Shakespeare, 20, 24, 33, 34, 58, 59, 61, 75, 111, 116, 123, 131, 132, 144, 147, 168

"The Shakespeare Code," 24, 33, 58, 59, 61, 75, 111, 116, 123, 131, 144, 147

Sherlock, 59, 70, 72, 82, 83, 84, 91, 94, 129, 130, 133

Sherlock Holmes, 59, 70, 72, 84, 128-133, 140

Silence, 39, 97, 102, 106, 122, 138, 173

"Silence in the Library," 27, 32, 50, 81, 104, 170

Silurians, 19, 49, 95, 96, 106, 107

The Simpsons, 142, 162

Sixth Doctor, 27, 33, 43, 50, 55, 70, 111, 123, 127, 133, 142, 156, 163

Sliding Doors, 143

Slitheen, 14, 49, 65, 93, 106, 113

"Small Worlds," 131, 154

"Smith and Jones," 80, 89, 91, 103, 106, 142, 148, 169

"The Snowmen," 15, 50, 57, 84, 98, 103, 130, 139, 142, 147, 153, 155

"Something Borrowed," 21, 127

"The Sontaran Strategem," 42, 98

Sontarans, 32, 49, 50, 95, 96, 98, 106, 113

"The Sound of Drums," 31, 99, 149

"Spearhead from Space," 97, 178

spoilers, 29-30

Star Trek, 35, 54, 57, 117-119, 122, 148, 162

Star Wars, 119-121, 163, 165

"State of Decay," 150

Steampunk, 66, 140

Stetson, 68-69

Steven Moffat, 10, 11, 15, 20, 23, 25, 30, 32, 44, 56, 57, 63, 70, 75, 81-84, 89, 91-95, 97, 101, 109, 111, 115, 118, 120, 122, 126, 130, 135, 136, 145, 146, 165, 173, 196

"The Stolen Earth," 21, 23, 48, 80, 151, 173

"The Stones of Blood," 152

Strax, 107, 124, 130

Supernatural, 162

Survivors, 117

Susan Foreman, 15, 19, 26, 50, 70, 85, 110, 175

Sycorax, 49, 65, 106, 147

Sylvester McCoy, 51, 127, 163, 175

"The Talons of Weng-Chiang," 72, 85, 99, 128-131

TARDIS, 9, 13, 14, 21, 23-29, 33, 47, 50, 51, 55-59, 61, 64, 73, 89, 91, 95, 99-104, 111- 113, 116, 121, 125-126, 133, 140, 159, 162-166, 171, 173 technology, 9, 10, 23, 34, 41-44, 81, 116, 136

Tegan Jovanka, 70, 98, 100, 113, 176

television, 8-11, 14, 16, 17, 22, 24, 28, 32, 33, 37, 39-44, 46, 47, 51, 52, 54, 57, 59, 80-83, 86-88, 97, 104, 108, 110-112, 116-117, 125, 139, 140-142, 147, 152, 159, 166, 168, 174, 191

"The Temptation of Sarah Jane Smith," 73, 149

Tenth Doctor, 11, 21-24, 27, 42, 50-51, 56-59, 63, 67, 69, 86, 87, 102, 103, 113, 118, 120-124, 128, 133, 136, 137, 142, 148, 153, 156, 157, 161- 164

The Terminator, 122, 144, 147

"Terror of the Zygons," 106

Terry Nation, 59, 117, 121, 129

The Grand, 79

"The Wheel in Space," 120

"They Keep Killing Suzie," 151

Third Doctor, 16, 46, 50, 66, 93, 97, 113, 118, 127, 138, 146, 153, 161

Time Agents, 99

"Time Crash," 14, 21, 59, 95, 100

Time Lord Rock, 10, 55, 158-159

Time Lords, 18, 19, 21, 22, 23, 37, 50, 63, 85, 97, 99, 100, 116, 121, 150

"The Time Monster," 37, 151-153

Time of the Angels, 99, 106, 138, 147

The Time Traveler's Wife, 146

Time War, 18, 19, 22, 25, 26, 37, 112

"Timelash," 133

Tom Baker, 54, 56, 66, 68, 92, 101, 127, 130, 163, 164, 175

"Tomb of the Cybermen," 101

"Tooth and Claw," 47, 71, 100, 104, 124, 135, 145, 150, 170

Torchwood, 10, 21, 42, 77, 79, 80, 88-93, 99, 101, 104, 106, 107, 110, 112-114, 119, 131- 134, 141, 142, 151, 154, 160, 170, 193

Toshiko Sato, 89, 123

Trenzalore, 28, 108

"The Trial of a Time Lord," 22

Trickster, 114, 137

Trickster's Brigade, 114

"Turn Left," 143, 160, 168

The Turn of the Screw, 136

Twelfth Doctor, 11, 21, 89

Twilight Zone, 140

Twitter, 45

"The Underwater Menace," 37, 152

"Underworld," 154-155

"The Unearthly Child," 47, 50, 99, 164

"The Unicorn and the Wasp," 84, 85, 133, 161, 171

UNIT, 37, 46, 54, 62, 63, 93, 98, 99, 102, 113, 146, 171
"The Unquiet Dead," 58, 70, 77, 93, 98, 104, 134, 137, 138
"Utopia," 22, 111, 171
vampires, 107, 150, 154
"The Vampires of Venice," 13, 87, 90, 146, 170, 171
Van Gogh, 34, 71, 146
Vastra, 57, 97, 107, 108, 130, 170
"The Vault of Secrets," 114
"Vengeance on Varos," 43, 97
Vespiforms, 49
Victorian, 42, 58, 68, 70, 71, 72, 103, 108, 129, 130, 136, 140
"Victory of the Daleks," 84, 106, 120
"Vincent and the Doctor," 34, 106, 169-171
"Voyage of the Damned," 90, 96, 136, 137, 143, 151
Wales, 89, 167-170, 172
"War Games," 90
War of the Worlds, 122, 129
"Warriors' Gate," 99
"The Waters of Mars," 103, 105, 145, 170

The Weakest Link, 40, 85, 141
"The Web of Fear," 17, 140
"The Wedding of River Song," 30, 31, 60, 105, 107, 137, 138, 145, 153, 168-171
Weeping Angels, 84, 108, 137, 147, 162, 173
Wendy Padbury, 90, 176
werewolves, 150, 154
What Not To Wear, 85
"Whatever Happened to Sarah Jane?," 37
Why Don't You?, 39
Wilfred Mott, 63, 89, 90, 103, 105, 171, 172
William Hartnell, 66, 127, 164, 175
Winnie-the-Pooh, 136
Winston Churchill, 106
Wizards vs Aliens, 78
Wolfsbane, 37, 150
World of Warcraft, 165
World War Z, 89
X-Files, 141, 142
Yana, 90
Yeti, 153
You Are Not Alone, 105
YouTube, 30, 56, 156, 166
Zoe Heriot, 32, 90, 102, 120, 152, 176

About the Author

Valerie Estelle Frankel has won a Dream Realm Award, an Indie Excellence Award, and a *USA Book News* National Best Book Award for her *Henry Potty* parodies. She's the author of many books on pop culture, including *From Girl to Goddess: The Heroine's Journey in Myth and Legend, Buffy and the Heroine's Journey, Winning the Game of Thrones: The Host of Characters and their Agendas, Katniss the Cattail: An Unauthorized Guide to Names and Symbols in The Hunger Games, An Unexpected Parody, Teaching with Harry Potter, Harry Potter: Still Recruiting,* and *Doctor Who and the Hero's Journey.* Once a lecturer at San Jose State University, she's a frequent speaker on fantasy, myth, and pop culture. Come explore her latest research at VEFrankel.com.